PIATTI

PIATTI

Plates and
Platters
for Sharing,
Inspired
by Italy

*From James Beard
Award–winning author*

Stacy Adimando

Photographs by
Linda Pugliese

Library of Congress Cataloging-in-Publication Data:

Names: Adimando, Stacy, author.
Title: Piatti / by Stacy Adimando.
Description: San Francisco : Chronicle Books, [2019] | Includes index.
Identifiers: LCCN 2018030263 | ISBN 9781452169576 (hardcover : alk. paper)
Subjects: LCSH: Cooking, Italian. | Seasonal cooking. | LCGFT: Cookbooks.
Classification: LCC TX723 .A35 2019 | DDC 641.5945—dc23
LC record available at https://lccn.loc.gov/2018030263

Manufactured in China

MIX
Paper from
responsible sources
FSC™ C008047
FSC
www.fsc.org

Design by Vanessa Dina
Prop styling by Paige Hicks
Food styling by Stacy Adimando

10 9 8 7 6 5 4 3 2 1

Microplane is a registered trademark of Grace Manufacturing, Inc. Weck is a
registered trademark of J. WECK GMBH & CO.

Chronicle books and gifts are available at special quantity discounts to corporations,
professional associations, literacy programs, and other organizations. For details
and discount information, please contact our corporate/premiums department at
corporatesales@chroniclebooks.com or at 1-800-759-0190.

Chronicle Books LLC
680 Second Street
San Francisco, California 94107
www.chroniclebooks.com

For my family,
past, present, and
future.

Braised Artichokes with Pistachio
Pesto and Burrata (page 129)

Grilled Crostini
(page 39)

Crispy Prosciutto or
Salami Chips (page 124)

INSPIRAZIONE

Years ago, when my Italian grandparents were still alive, I told them I wanted to find and meet some of our distant family in Italy. "My relatives are in Reggio Calabria," one of my grandfathers used to say, referring to the city on the outermost point of Italy's so-called boot. But because he never said anything more, I had always assumed it would be difficult to locate them. I braced for what I guessed would be a committed search involving digging through government records and old family trees. Twenty-four hours later, I had all of their phone numbers and addresses in Italy.

The easy thing about visiting this part of my family was they all lived in the same house in Reggio: four branches of family in one four-family building, the eldest grandmother living on the bottom floor and the youngest son living on the top floor, a very traditional Italian setup. There was a big garden with chickens beside the house, tiled floors and crucifixes everywhere, and every branch of the family had another son named Matteo.

The first night, they took me out to a local restaurant for dinner. I remember writing my mother back in the States over email, telling her I was surprised they had taken me out and not cooked dinner at home. "I get the feeling they don't make a big fuss about cooking?" I wrote with confusion, and admittedly a little disappointment.

The next day, my great-aunts said they wanted to cook me "a little lunch," which I also wrote about to my mother. "They brought out a

spread of salami and cheeses, olives, some oil-preserved eggplant, marinated mushrooms, a dish of spicy beans, and a mountain of fried pork and veal meatballs with bread," I wrote. Because I was navigating the experience with only my mediocre Italian, "I thought that was the end of the meal, so I ate a *lot*." Silly me. After that, there were thick pork sausages and soft-cooked peppers in a pool of olive oil, an entire eggplant Parmigiana with layers of boiled eggs and prosciutto hidden between the eggplant slices, breaded veal cutlets each as wide as a frying pan, a giant bowl of fettuccini with swordfish, capers, and tomatoes, and a dessert—the most gargantuan almond cake I've ever seen.

This kind of over-the-top feast was my Italian-relative dream come true. But they had had me—before the pasta came out, before the cream-filled cake—at the antipasti.

In my travels around Italy, my fondness for this style of food—abundant platters, often served a few at a time, some warm and others at room temperature—has remained a constant. At a restaurant called Zia Pina's in Palermo, Sicily, an antipasti buffet as long as a bowling alley is the first thing that greeted me at the door. There were heaps of golden bread crumbs stuffed inside soft-cooked vegetables, green olive salad with cubed ham and coarsely shredded carrots, potatoes falling apart in a pool of oil, tender red peppers, and a spatula dangling from a baking dish filled with oily eggplant. We spent so much time picking out our antipasti, then lapping up the sauces and crumbs with a crusty loaf of bread, we nearly forgot to order mains. In the *osterias* of Rome, nothing can stand between me and a platter of salty fried *artichokes alla romana*, creamy *fagiolini con le cotiche* (beans in a puddle of olive oil with morsels of crispy pork), or *fiore di zucca*, fried zucchini flowers usually filled with anchovies and cheese. So often, my most romantic memories of a new region would include these first bites we ate, when the table was just beginning to buzz with conversation, and no one yet knew where the night would take us.

Back home, I wondered why this type of grazing couldn't last all night. Fast-forward to a recent day in my Brooklyn neighborhood, one of the last fall days my husband and I knew would be warm enough to host friends and neighbors in our backyard, when we decided to throw a party. "Come over," we told friends, "bring whomever you want, there will be snacks." We put bottles of sparkling wine on ice in a big tin bucket we use in the garden. As friends arrived, we shucked clams and oysters in the kitchen and brought them out back on a haphazardly crushed plate of ice. We draped fruit with some of the peppery cured lardo we had in our meat drawer, and cracked open homemade jars of marinated artichoke hearts and mushrooms. And we simmered—in the oven in the background, while glasses clinked and guests had already begun nibbling—pork I made a special trip to the butcher for, in its own fat and juices with loads of bay leaves and a hint of citrus peel.

Most of our friends could hardly believe I had characterized this as "snacks." But it felt natural to my husband and me, as this—a spoil-your-dinner spread of too much food, laid out casually on big, pretty platters—is how we like to eat and entertain.

There is plenty that inspires the way I cook, from a formal culinary training and years working as a food writer and editor, to a certain natural-born disposition that will lead me always to prefer a vegetable to meat (my husband feels the opposite). But if I must pick one primary source of inspiration, cliché or not, it's Italy: my upbringing as an Italian American, my incessant journeys to the country, and the way a meal there ends up being a little of everything, served slowly over time, in a quantity you didn't think you could eat.

I believe this way of eating—grazing casually over a series of plates big and small—is a wonderful way to eat and entertain at home, not just something we should experience as a first course when traveling in a foreign country. Those moments, when the initial platters of warm food hit the table, and the flush of alcohol is just beginning to hit our cheeks, might arguably be the best moments of any meal. Today, I like to focus on these moments, stretching them to last the whole evening, when I serve and entertain.

A friend gave me the best compliment after leaving our house on that fall day. She said, "You make me want to throw a party."

That's the idea.

The Italian Connection and Departure

Born to a big American family of southern Italian lineage, I learned nothing of moderation as a cook and hostess. Throughout my upbringing, whenever a large meal, such as a holiday feast, was hosted at my house, we began with a signature vegetable, meat, and cheese spread: mounds of marinated eggplant, piles of pickles, stacks of greasy salami, plus roasted peppers, cheese, and bread. I learned to make antipasti from my big Italian family and my trips to Italy, and, to me, it means a hearty, overly generous compilation of colorful, textural, help-yourself platters.

Although Italy's big, bountiful antipasti are what inspire the recipes in this book most, the plates you'll find on these pages are not strictly Italian recipes, nor meant to be eaten strictly as a first course. Rather, they're made in the spirit of the old-world Italian spreads: generous, abundant, rustic, and seasonal; never puny or precious finger food; and over-the-top enough to fill you up. I've used the model of Italy's antipasti as a jumping-off point for creating dishes and combinations that work for modern cooks anywhere, and that can be served individually as a beginning course or snack, or in tandem as a meal.

Somehow, in America, the go-to foods we graze on have remained mind-bogglingly stagnant since the very idea of the cheese and charcuterie board hopped over the pond. Unfailingly, when tasked with bringing an appetizer or putting out a snack for guests, most people—including accomplished home cooks and chefs—rely on crackers or bread and the classic but expected staples of charcuterie, sliced cheeses, nuts, and olives. It is shocking that in a time when cooks and diners everywhere are singing the praises of vibrant seasonal ingredients and creative, colorful ways to prepare and serve them, somehow not a single one of these trends has trickled down to the platters we put out for guests.

I also find that what follows an antipasti-style menu is typically some kind of main course and sides in America—or *primi* and *secondi* in Italy—which, at home, can often be formal feeling and disparate from the casual snacks, not to mention too much food and work for the host. What I've done instead is focus on simple large and small plates that can either be the starting bites or carry through as the main event.

Because I did learn to cook from my Italian grandmothers, grandfathers, and parents, and because I believe deeply in carrying on traditional recipes from our families and heritage, it came naturally to write down the things we make in the ways we have always made them. Much of this book is dedicated to my family's recipes or my own twists on them, and most other dishes are inspired by the regions of Italy and their foods, which vary widely. There are a few outliers, less rigidly Italian in ingredients or preparation but that I created in the spirit of the country's rustic, simple, and filling dishes.

The recipes are designed to be made quickly and easily enough to tackle more than one in a day, many even shortly before guests arrive. There really are no rules about what to serve or how to serve it, but there are some helpful pillars.

A Few Antipasti Guidelines

Classically, in Italy, antipasti is a no-pressure spread of whatever you have in the house, intended to kick-start appetites at the table, express generosity, and settle everyone into a gathering. The offerings change from region to region, and event to event, but some common themes are a loyalty to the seasons, a focus on vegetables and meager proteins, and a rustic and simplistic style. Antipasti should not be about formality or fussiness, but food made with love, with ease, and often in advance.

The cooks of Italy seem born knowing the secrets to pulling off an impressive spread. So, my best antipasti tips take a cue from them: Make some things from scratch, but add store-bought ingredients to fill the gaps. Create foods that can be made ahead and taste great warm and at room temperature. Serve some in little plates and others strewn across boards, some in piles, some in stacks, others in jars, some with spoons, others with knives, and still others with crusty bread or crackers for dipping, dunking, and scooping. Think about color. Think about texture. Think about surprising people. Fall back on foods you've preserved in advance—in oils and vinegars, or by drying or curing—then complement them with fresh foods plucked from markets or the garden. Offer good bread, and great wine, and plan for people to consume far more of both than you'd expect.

Something should always be spilling over the sides of an antipasto platter. Everything, really, should be a little messy. It should feel humble, but generous, and inspired by what's in the market that week. The spread of dishes should vary from finger foods to fork-and-knife platters, but no one dish should overwhelm the others. Think of it as a buffet of sorts, but the kind the most gifted of Italian grandmas could cook and most inspiring of friends could arrange. Feel free to apply your personal style.

Serving Your Antipasti

So much of the appeal of great antipasti is seeing it laid out decoratively among platters, plates, bowls, and boards. The charming intermingling of dishes—the ingredients leaning up against one another, textures contrasting, colors popping—should be enhanced by the beautiful serving objects beneath them.

Our world's obsession with food is more visually driven than ever, and there is no spread of food more fun to make and no food photo more fun to take than that of a tabletop abundantly adorned with lots of foods to graze on. Mix serving vessels like well-loved roasting pans and weathered baking sheets, pretty cake stands, mismatched plates, crinkled butcher paper, scalloped tart pans, vintage cutting boards, metal or ceramic trays, gold-rimmed platters, marble boards, rustic butcher blocks, salad bowls, enamelware, and more.

Whatever style you love, antipasti is the best excuse to dust off even special-occasion tableware and get to work setting up a dreamy spread.

Antipasti Building Blocks

With a few simple elements always at the ready—like jars of preserved or marinated vegetables, or long-storing crackers or breadsticks—you'll have the makings of an antipasti spread that takes almost no effort at serving time. I keep at least a few of these foods tucked away in my refrigerator throughout the seasons to pull out whenever there's little to eat in the house or people are coming over.

Oil-Preserved Vegetables

Italians, and my family, have a great love of oil-preserved vegetables as antipasti—from peppers to mushrooms to eggplant. Qualified as *sott'olio*, which means "under oil," this style of vegetable is delicious served on its own, and also makes an incredible addition to a cheese board or topping for charcuterie sandwiches.

Pickles

In Italy, pickled vegetables are usually sour and lightly sweet, and are often eaten alongside something fatty, such as cured meats. I like that many of the pickled, or *sott'aceto*, products from there start with bold, clean vinegars, tempered with a little sugar (or sometimes a lot) and some seasonings. I use distilled white vinegar for most basic pickling: unlike white wine and red wine vinegars, it's inexpensive in large quantities and the flavor, intensity, and quality do not vary much among brands.

Pickled and Marinated Vegetables

In many of the smaller towns and villages of Italy, cooking is first about going out and seeing what there is to buy that day from the vegetable vendors. Many families, including my relatives in Calabria, also keep a substantial garden—or at least a few lovingly tended planters on the balcony—from which a simple meal or antipasti can be plucked and prepared at a moment's notice.

Because gardens grow quiet in the winter, and not all of us have them (yet), preserved vegetables are a way to keep a wider variety of vegetable antipasti within arm's reach year-round. Though even in Italy, I'm not sure as many cooks and families preserve their own vegetables as was once the case; all over the country you can continue to buy (or, in my case, smuggle home) myriad preserved vegetables—sometimes jarred, and sometimes simply stored in tubs of golden olive oil behind the case at delis and markets with big metal serving ladles. Many of these make perfect antipasti just pulled from the jar with the remnants of the herby oil still clinging to them. In parts of Italy, these unfussy preserves, along with salumi, cheeses, or, if you're in southern Italy, anchovies, might be known as *companatico*, a word that means "things that go with bread." I love this concept.

Store-bought versions of preserved vegetables can be exquisite, and you can find great ones anywhere at gourmet markets and specialty shops. But it is fun and satisfying to store your own, be they bathed in oil, pickled, marinated, or lightly fermented. A colorful stock of even a few of these long-keeping jars lining your cupboards or refrigerator shelves can do wonders for your ability to entertain with ease, or just come up with something to graze on when you have little else in the house. Plus, the pretty jars go a long way in making me feel like I live in the Italian countryside.

While almost any hearty vegetable can make a delicious and viable candidate for pickling, marinating, or oil preserving, I tend to gravitate toward those in season for short amounts of time—cherry peppers in late summer and fall, rainbow-colored radishes in winter, and baby artichokes any time I can find them fresh. This way, when I'm nostalgic for seasons past or impatient for those to come, I can crack open a jar. Add a loaf of bread and some wine and you have a delightful antipasto.

Oil-Preserved Cherry Peppers (page 21)

Pickled Chiles (page 25)

Oil-Preserved Eggplant with
Sage and Chile (page 20)

Pickled Red Onions (page 26)

Radish Giardiniera (page 28)

Classic Giardiniera (page 27)

OIL-PRESERVED EGGPLANT

with sage and chile

A version of this preparation is the centerpiece of my family's holiday antipasti, served in heaps among slices of provolone, tomatoes, salami, and marinated mushrooms. Some cooks only salt the eggplant first, leaving it out on their kitchen counter for days to expel every last drop of water. But to maintain some plumpness, add flavor, and spare my kitchen counter space, I lightly cook the pieces in vinegar after a quick salting and before jarring. It's important to use medium, not large, eggplant to prevent sogginess and minimize seeds. This eggplant can (and ideally should) be prepared up to a few weeks or months ahead.

4 lb [1.8 kg] Italian eggplant, about 4 medium eggplants, peeled and sliced lengthwise into ¼-in- [6-mm-] thick strands

3 Tbsp kosher salt, plus more as needed

1 cup [240 ml] distilled white vinegar

Juice of 1 lemon

2 large garlic cloves, peeled

2 to 4 fresh sage leaves, or a few fresh marjoram sprigs

1 medium-heat red chile, such as Fresno, halved lengthwise

1 to 2 cups [240 to 480 ml] extra-virgin olive oil

MAKES 2½ CUPS [500 G EGGPLANT]

See photo page 18

Place the eggplant pieces in a large strainer and set it in the sink. Sprinkle generously with 3 Tbsp of salt, tossing until all the strands are well seasoned. Let sit for a few hours, squeezing the eggplant firmly on occasion to release all the water possible. If the eggplant is not letting out much water, you may need more salt.

When the eggplant has softened, looks moistened, and has had most of its water squeezed out, after about 1 hour, take out a large pot or skillet. In it, combine the eggplant, vinegar, lemon juice, and 1 cup [240 ml] of water and bring to a simmer over medium heat. Simmer, tossing the eggplant frequently with tongs, until softened slightly more and fully saturated, 1 to 2 minutes (do not overcook, as the eggplant will be soggy).

Drain immediately in a large strainer and let the eggplant cool significantly. Again, squeeze out the excess liquid. To get the final bits of liquid out, place the eggplant in a clean, thin kitchen towel and wring it out.

Transfer the eggplant to an appropriate-size jar or two. Distribute the garlic, herbs, and chile throughout. Fill each jar to the top with olive oil so the eggplant is completely submerged. Let sit for a few minutes, tilting and swiveling the jar a bit to help the oil settle. Add more oil, if needed, to submerge. Tightly seal and let sit at room temperature for 1 day. Add more olive oil, if needed, to cover. Keep refrigerated until ready to use, up to 2 months. Remove the jar and let the oil come fully to room temperature before serving.

OIL-PRESERVED CHERRY PEPPERS

In Italy and Italian-American markets, you will often see preserved cherry peppers stuffed with prosciutto, cheese, tuna, or anchovies—a ubiquitous antipasto. This recipe is for plain peppers, which you can serve on their own alongside cheeses, seafood, or meat antipasti, or stuff with fillings. Try them with the Grilled Shell-On Shrimp with Parsley and Ginger Salmoriglio (page 170) or the Mini "Porchetta" with Radish Giardiniera and Pork Fat Toasts (page 202).

7 oz [200 g] cherry peppers,
about 20 medium

½ cup [120 ml] distilled white vinegar

1½ tsp kosher salt

½ tsp sugar

4 sprigs fresh oregano

1 large garlic clove, peeled

1 cup [240 ml] extra-virgin olive oil,
plus more as needed

MAKES 1 PINT [100 G PEPPERS]

See photo page 18

Using the tip of a paring knife, cut around the cherry pepper stems to remove the stems and some of the seeds. Continue to use the tip of the knife to hollow out the peppers, removing the remaining seeds and ribs.

In a small saucepan over medium-high heat, combine the vinegar, ½ cup [120 ml] of water, the salt, sugar, 2 oregano sprigs, and the garlic. Bring to a strong simmer and add the cleaned peppers. Continue to simmer until slightly tenderized but not at all soggy, about 3 minutes. Strain, reserving the peppers and garlic (save the brine for another use, if desired). Drain the peppers upside down on a paper towel-lined plate until completely dry.

Transfer the dry peppers to a pint-size [480-ml] jar and distribute the remaining 2 oregano sprigs and the reserved garlic clove throughout. Fill the jar to the top with olive oil so the peppers are completely submerged. Let sit for a few minutes, tilting and swiveling the jar a bit to help the oil settle. Add more oil, if needed, to submerge. Tightly seal, and let sit at room temperature for 1 day. Add more olive oil, if needed, to cover. Keep refrigerated until ready to use, up to 2 months. Remove the jar and let the oil come fully to room temperature before serving or filling the peppers.

GINGERED CHERRY TOMATO CONFIT

This process of slow cooking and preserving tomatoes in oil—borrowed from the French—softens them into a juicy, pulpy topping of sorts. This recipe is intended for peak-season tomatoes, which will retain all their intense sweetness and flavor in the oil. Serve atop Grilled Crostini (page 39), alongside mozzarella or burrata, with cooked polenta, grains, or breads, such as Olive Oil Cornmeal Cake with Rosemary and Honey (page 146). Or spoon over vegetables, like grilled baby zucchini; meats, such as Braised Pork with Garlic, Bay Leaves, and Orange Peel (page 191); or frittatas, like the Broccolini Frittata with Torn, Oil-Packed Anchovies or Grated Cheese (page 90).

14 oz [400 g] cherry tomatoes [about 2 heaping cups], preferably a mix of colors, shapes, and sizes

2 medium garlic cloves, peeled

1 sprig fresh thyme or a few large fresh basil leaves

½ tsp finely grated, peeled fresh ginger

1 cup [240 ml] extra-virgin olive oil, plus more as needed

¼ tsp sea salt or kosher salt

MAKES ABOUT 1 PINT
[1½ CUPS OR 350 G TOMATOES]

Preheat the oven to 350°F [180°C].

Halve most of the cherry tomatoes through the stems and leave very small ones whole. Place the tomatoes, garlic, thyme, ginger, olive oil, and sea salt in a pie plate or medium baking dish, with most of the cut sides of the tomatoes facing up. Be sure the tomatoes are completely covered by the oil.

Bake until the skins look wrinkled and the tomatoes look softened and juicy, 30 to 35 minutes. Remove and let cool slightly.

Transfer the mixture to a jar or storage container and let cool completely. At this point you can use some of the tomatoes (or even just some of the oil) immediately, or cover and refrigerate until ready to use, up to 1 month. (If storing, be sure the tomatoes are completely covered in the olive oil at all times, adding more, if needed, at any point.) Bring to room temperature before eating, or reheat the mixture gently on the stovetop, if desired.

GARLIC CONFIT

A jar of this in the kitchen will never go to waste. Garlic cloves are gently heated in olive oil until they become silky, sweet, and subtle tasting. Purée them into dips, soups, or sauces; spoon them atop cooked vegetables or meats; or serve a little bowl of them on their own alongside any antipasto.

4 garlic heads, cloves separated and peeled [about 1¼ cups, or 160 g]

1 cup [240 ml] extra-virgin olive oil, plus more as needed

5 black peppercorns

1 bay leaf or small sprig fresh rosemary

¼ tsp kosher salt

MAKES ABOUT 1½ CUPS
[¾ CUP OR 130 G GARLIC]

Preheat the oven to 350°F [180°C].

Meanwhile, in a small (6-in, or 15-cm) baking dish, combine the garlic, olive oil, peppercorns, bay leaf, and salt. Be sure the garlic is completely covered by the oil.

Place the baking dish on a small baking sheet, and roast until the cloves are softened, aromatic, and lightly browned in places but still holding their shape, about 45 minutes. Remove and let cool slightly.

Transfer the mixture to a jar or storage container and let cool completely. At this point you can use some of the garlic (or even just some of the oil) immediately, or cover and keep refrigerated until ready to use, up to about 6 weeks. Discard at any sign of mold. (If storing, be sure the garlic cloves are completely covered in the olive oil at all times, adding more, if needed, at any point.) Bring to room temperature before eating, or reheat the mixture gently on the stovetop, if desired.

BASIC BRINE

for pickled vegetables

This is a recipe intended for immediate use in basic jarring, *not* airtight canning for long-term stability. So, for food-safety purposes, it is important to store all pickled vegetables made from this book in the refrigerator. Once refrigerated, they will keep indefinitely.

¾ cup [180 ml] distilled white vinegar

¼ cup [60 ml] white wine vinegar

2 tsp kosher salt

½ tsp sugar

8 to 10 black peppercorns

1 large garlic clove, peeled

MAKES 2 CUPS [480 ML]

In a small saucepan over medium-high heat, combine all the ingredients with 1 cup [240 ml] of water. Bring to a strong simmer, stirring until the salt and sugar dissolve.

PICKLED CHILES

Hot peppers are used fresh in pastas and antipasti most prevalently in the south of Italy, where they grow easily and abundantly. This recipe, which preserves them for use at any time, will work with any firm *peperoncini* (small chiles) you like, such as jalapeños, Fresnos, or serranos. I thinly slice them so I can use them right out of the jar, but halving the peppers lengthwise is enough to allow the brine to work its magic, or you can go as far as finely dicing them.

6 oz [170 g] sliced fresh chiles
[about 6 medium chiles, or 2 cups]

1 recipe Basic Brine for Pickled Vegetables (facing page), hot

MAKES TWO 8-OZ [240-ML] JARS

See photo page 18

Divide the sliced chiles between two 8-oz [240-ml] jars. Pour enough of the hot brine over the top to fill each jar completely and submerge the chiles. Let rest until completely cooled. Cover the jars and refrigerate for at least 1 day before using. These will keep for up to 4 months in the refrigerator.

PICKLED RED ONIONS

Red onions, or *cippole rosse*, are sometimes eaten grilled or simmered *agrodolce* (sweet and sour) on their own in Italy—especially in parts such as Tropea, where the region's famous red onions are dramatically sweet. Admittedly, you rarely see them strictly pickled, but I love to use this preparation to add a puckery sourness to the onions and use them for topping fish or vegetable dishes. You can also remove them from the jar, heat them lightly, if desired, and toss them with dried Italian herbs and some olive oil before using. Cut the onions into wedges, thin slices, or a fine dice to change up your pickles' texture.

4 cups [425 g] thinly sliced red onion wedges

1 recipe Basic Brine for Pickled Vegetables
(page 24), still hot

MAKES ABOUT 2 PINTS [400 G ONIONS]

See photo page 19

Divide the onions between two pint-size [470-ml] jars. Pour enough of the hot brine over the top to fill each jar completely and submerge the onions. Let rest until completely cooled. Cover the jars and refrigerate for at least 1 day before using. Save any remaining brine for another use. These will keep for up to 4 months in the refrigerator.

CLASSIC GIARDINIERA

Giardiniera, which means "gardener" in Italian, is a traditional pickled vegetable assortment that can be used finely chopped as a tangy garnish, or more coarsely chopped and served as antipasto alongside something rich. There are no strict rules for which vegetables the mix contains, but the traditional versions usually have cauliflower, carrots, peppers, and, sometimes, celery and chiles. My recipe is not as cloyingly sweet as some of the store-bought versions. I adore a few spoonfuls with Italian sandwiches (like the "Six-Foot Sub" Baguettes, page 198) or alongside grilled or seared sausages.

1 large [3½-oz, or 100-g] carrot, peeled and sliced

1¼ cups [4 oz, or 140 g] cauliflower florets, broken into small pieces

1 [1¼-oz, or 35-g] celery stalk with leaves, sliced on the diagonal

1 small [7-oz, or 200-g] red bell pepper, chopped into 2-in [5-cm] pieces

Few slices fresh chile or store-bought pickled peperoncini (optional)

BRINE

1 cup [240 ml] distilled white vinegar

¼ cup [60 ml] white wine vinegar

1½ tsp kosher salt

1 tsp sugar

½ tsp dried basil

½ tsp dried oregano

½ tsp dried parsley

2 large garlic cloves, peeled

MAKES ABOUT 1 QUART
[ABOUT 365 G VEGETABLES]

See photo page 19

Before you begin, have the vegetables fully prepared.

PREPARE THE BRINE: In a medium saucepan over medium-high heat, combine the vinegars, 1 cup [240 ml] of water, the salt, sugar, dried herbs, and garlic. Bring to a strong simmer, stirring until the salt and sugar dissolve.

Add the vegetables and chile (if using) and simmer until the carrots are softened slightly but still retain a bite, 2 to 3 minutes. (The vegetables will continue to cook in the liquid once the heat is turned off.) Turn off the heat and let cool slightly.

Transfer the vegetables and as much of the brine as can fit into a quart-size [480-ml] jar. Let cool completely. Seal the jar and refrigerate for at least 1 day, and up to a few months, before using. Shake the jar to redistribute the seasonings as needed before using.

RADISH GIARDINIERA

I think of this as a new-age *giardiniera*: It's the same brine used for the Classic Giardiniera (page 27), but with a more precious array of winter or spring vegetables, like mixed-color radishes and the tiniest baby rainbow carrots. It has more bite than classic *giardiniera* because of the peppery-tasting radishes. I like it with roasted pork, sausages, or something else warm, meaty, and comforting.

VEGETABLES

12 oz [340 g] mixed baby root vegetables, such as winter radishes (black, purple, watermelon, or a mix) and multicolored carrots

BRINE

1 cup [240 ml] distilled white vinegar

¼ cup [60 ml] white wine vinegar

1½ tsp kosher salt

1 tsp sugar

½ tsp dried basil

½ tsp dried oregano

½ tsp dried parsley

2 large garlic cloves, peeled

MAKES 1½ PINTS [340 G VEGETABLES]

See photo page 19

PREPARE THE VEGETABLES: Peel any rough skins away and discard. For large winter radishes, halve or quarter them lengthwise depending on their size, then thinly slice. For the carrots or baby carrots, cut them into a size you like that will cook at a similar rate to the radish slices (I like thin slices on the diagonal for regular carrots, or quartering tiny carrots such as Thumbelinas). Place the vegetables in a quart-size [480 ml] jar.

PREPARE THE BRINE: In a small saucepan over medium-high heat, combine the vinegars, 1 cup [240 ml] of water, the salt, sugar, dried herbs, and garlic. Bring to a strong simmer, stirring until the salt and sugar dissolve.

Remove from the heat and pour enough hot brine over the vegetables to submerge them fully. Let cool completely. Seal the jar and refrigerate for at least 1 day, or up to a few months, before using. Shake the jar to redistribute the seasonings as needed before using.

DRIED CHILI OIL

Though many infused olive oils in Italy use whole, dried chiles, using crushed flakes instead means you don't have to wait weeks for the peppers to impart their flavor. The heat of this oil can range dramatically depending on the chili flakes you have, so start sparingly when drizzling the finished oil atop foods. I love to use the oil and flakes generously drizzled atop seared broccoli, sautéed broccoli rabe, or sweet roasted squash, as well as hard-boiled eggs, bocconcini, or pretty much any dish in this book.

1 Tbsp plus 1 tsp dried chili flakes

⅓ cup [80 ml] extra-virgin olive oil, or more as desired

1 garlic clove, peeled and lightly smashed

1 sprig fresh thyme

MAKES ABOUT ⅓ CUP [80 ML]

Add the chili flakes to a medium heatproof bowl and set it next to the stove.

In a small saucepan over low heat, combine the olive oil, garlic, and thyme. Cook until the garlic smells aromatic, 5 to 8 minutes.

Pour the oil over the chili flakes and stir for 60 seconds to combine. Let cool completely. Taste and adjust the oil quantity as desired (adding more will dilute the heat). Use immediately, if desired, or within 2 days at room temperature. Keep refrigerated for up to 2 weeks and bring to room temperature or gently reheat before using.

Chile Condiments

In parts of Italy's sun-bleached south, it is rare to visit a country house that does not have a string of *peperoncini* hanging outside the door to dry. The region in general is home to a few chile festivals, and more than a few types of hot pepper condiments, from *pilacca*, a panfried chile and garlic sauce, to *olio santo*, a chile-infused olive oil. It's worth having some kind of chile topping in your pantry or fridge for spooning on antipasti at will.

SPICY PEPPER RELISH

Calabria has the finest chile paste in Italy. Many jarred versions are lightly fermented before being packaged, giving them a wonderful tangy, savory, and lightly sour note. The fermentation also helps preserve the peppers, meaning this pepper paste, if used regularly, will last in your refrigerator for months. It does take time to make, however, so be prepared to wait at least 5 days before using.

This version of pepper relish has all the tanginess of the classic, but also a sweet fresh pepper flavor and juiciness. You can also make a yellow or orange pepper relish by playing around with the pepper varieties you find at the market.

1 lb [455 g] red bell peppers, coarsely chopped

6 oz [170 g] medium- to high-heat fresh red chiles, seeded

1 Tbsp kosher salt

MAKES ABOUT 1 PINT [625 G]

In a food processor, combine the bell peppers, chiles, and salt. Process into a lightly chunky paste. Transfer to a pint-size [480-ml] jar and place a piece of plastic wrap directly against the surface of the pepper paste; press all around to be sure the paste is completely covered all the way to the sides of the jar (this helps prevent mold growth). Cover with an airtight lid.

Set the jar in a clean, dark area that's not too warm and not too cool for about 5 days, opening the jar and stirring the paste (and tasting, if desired) once a day. It should start to taste gently sour after 5 days; leave for up to 7 days, if desired.

Discard the paste if you see any signs of mold growth. Otherwise, remove the plastic wrap, seal the jar well, and refrigerate. Use as desired, continuing to stir the paste occasionally. If stirred occasionally, this will keep for up to several months.

THE ANTIPASTI PANTRY

Having any of these store-bought staples on hand
can also help bulk up your antipasti offerings.

Oil-packed sardines, for serving with crackers or bread. Drizzle with a little vinegar, if desired, or add finely chopped herbs or dried raisins or currants before serving.

Oil-packed anchovies, for eating on their own or draping atop vegetables, frittatas, or serving on toasts. You can serve on a small, pretty plate in a pool of their own oil. If desired, add seasonings (think chili flakes, herbs, celery leaves, or a little vinegar).

Fruit preserves and marmalades, for spreading onto crackers or crostini, or eating with cheeses, cold meats, or ham. For something fancy, try fig jam, *cotognata*—a delicious Sicilian quince paste—or fancy marmalades like Alan Gray's small-batch Seville Orange and Scotch Marmalade from New York's Hudson Valley.

Good-quality, room-temperature butter, for accompanying bread of course, but also serving as a dip on its own for fritters, or with honey, herbs, or spices mixed in.

Extra-virgin olive oil, for brushing onto bread before grilling, marinating or preserving vegetables, or drizzling atop anything and everything. Italians also use it as a dip for raw vegetables.

Assorted nuts, for candying, spicing, drizzling with truffle oil, puréeing into pestos, or serving on their own. My grandfather loved to put out a big bowl of shell-on nuts and serve them (with a nutcracker) alongside raw fennel and tangerines.

Dried beans, for simmering and then serving with cooked greens or garlicky oil. You can soak dried beans in water overnight, drain them, then freeze in small portions so they're instantly ready to cook.

Garlic, for flavoring cooked foods, roasting or confiting into a sweet topping, or rubbing onto slices of bread before toasting or grilling.

Vinegars, for pickling, marinating, drizzling, or making vinaigrettes. I always keep on hand good red and white wine vinegars, an aged balsamic di Modena, and a big bottle of distilled white vinegar for pickling.

Canned tomatoes, for stewing seafood, crushing and layering between panfried eggplant slices, or as a dipping sauce for fried foods. I usually start with canned whole peeled tomatoes and break them down as needed.

Basic Crackers and Breads

Buono come il pane, "as good as bread," is the way Italians used to describe a dependable, good-hearted person. Bread is rarely missing on their tables, fundamental to everyday eating and entertaining, and a doorway into the history and nuances of the country's many regions. Although I adore a holey slab of focaccia and a rough-skinned, chewy loaf of ciabatta, you can find good recipes for the former anywhere, and good versions of the latter at most bakeries. The recipes listed here are not for yeasted loaves, but for their more simplistic cousins and siblings—flatbreads, crackers, and breadsticks—to serve with antipasti.

CARTA DI MUSICA

This paper-thin semolina flatbread was a staple of Sardinian shepherds who would travel with sheets of it while tending their herds (*carta di musica* almost never goes bad). Basically, a rustic free-form cracker, it is said to resemble the parchment papers on which sheet music was written—which is allegedly where it got its name.

Traditionally, the simple grain, salt, and water dough was rolled out and then placed in a scorching-hot oven where it puffed up into two layers. It was then sliced in half by an experienced baker to create single thin sheets. The method used here eliminates the need to slice the baking dough in half, turning out brittle, bubbly wafers instantly. Be sure to preheat your baking stone, baking steel, or a thick metal baking sheet thoroughly before making the crackers.

Carta di musica can last for weeks, so these crackers are perfect for rolling and baking ahead when you have time, and pulling out whenever friends come over. It's communal food, as everyone can break off many bits and bites from a few large slabs.

1 cup plus 1 Tbsp semolina (durum) flour [180 g]

1 cup plus 1 Tbsp unbleached all-purpose flour [137 g]

1¼ tsp kosher salt, plus more for seasoning

MAKES 12 TO 14 MEDIUM
[6- TO 8-IN, OR 15- TO 20-CM] PIECES

See photo page 40

In a large bowl, combine the flours and 1¼ tsp salt. Stir briefly with a fork to combine. Add ¾ cup [180 ml] of water and mix with a fork to incorporate. (The mixture will start to look chunky and crumbly.) Use your hands to squeeze the mixture into one big ball to form a dough, scooping and kneading all the pieces together repeatedly until a ball forms.

Turn out the dough onto a clean counter. If there are straggler grains of flour in the bowl, add them to the center of the dough ball and wrap them in the dough to incorporate. Knead for about 2 minutes, until the dough ball is more pliable and springy. Set aside.

Preheat the oven to 500°F [260°C] and set a rack in the top shelf. Place a sturdy metal baking sheet, pizza stone, or baking steel on the top rack to preheat.

Once preheated, pull off little pieces of dough about the size of a half ping-pong ball (start small until you get used to the dough). Smush the ball into a flatter shape (it doesn't matter if it's a circle or another shape). Using a rolling pin and *not* flouring the work surface (you want the dough to sort of stick to the surface as you roll), roll the dough, rotating it as needed and pressing it against the counter to help it stay steady, until it reaches the thinnest possible point before it breaks; if it tears in little places, that's okay. While it's at its thinnest [maybe 6 to 8 in, or 15 to 20 cm, long or wide], season it very lightly with more salt and rub the salt in using your fingers.

continued

Peel the dough piece off the counter and transfer to the preheated baking sheet or stone in the oven. Bake on the top rack until the dough is firm, blistered in places, and browned on the sides, 7 to 8 minutes. Meanwhile, roll out more pieces of dough, continuing to place them on the preheated pan or stone as you go. Continue this until all the dough is rolled, varying the sizes of the pieces as you desire.

Let cool on a cooling rack. Eat immediately or store in an airtight container for up to a few weeks.

Carta di Musica are delicious on their own or with toppings. See page 55 for this recipe with broiled Parmigiano, coppa, and chiles.

OLIVE OIL AND SEA SALT CRACKERS

with whole wheat

With a batch of these in the house, anything from a prepared spread to a nub of cheese can become an elegant antipasto. I use a mix of stone-ground whole-wheat and white flour to make the dough and brush these crackers generously with olive oil before baking. The dough will feel dry and tough when mixing, but it rolls and bakes beautifully. Be sure to remind people that you made these lovely crackers—otherwise they might never suspect it.

1¼ cups [162 g] unbleached all-purpose flour,
plus more as needed

¾ cup [100 g] coarsely ground
whole-wheat flour (such as stone-ground)

1 Tbsp extra-virgin olive oil,
plus more for brushing

1 tsp kosher salt

Flaky sea salt, for sprinkling

MAKES ABOUT 48

See photo page 41

In a large bowl, combine the flours, ½ cup plus 1 tsp of water [125 ml total], the olive oil, and kosher salt. Stir until a dough forms (the dough will feel stiff and relatively dry). Turn out the dough onto a clean work surface and knead until it feels elastic and looks mostly smooth, 10 to 15 minutes. If the dough becomes sticky at any point, sprinkle it with 1 tsp of all-purpose flour to help.

Place the dough back into the bowl and cover the bowl with plastic wrap. Set aside at room temperature for 1 hour. (The dough can also be refrigerated overnight at this point. Bring to room temperature before proceeding.)

Preheat the oven to 350°F [180°C] and line two baking sheets with parchment paper.

Transfer the dough to a lightly floured work surface and cut it into 4 equal wedges. Using a lightly floured rolling pin and working with one piece of dough at a time, roll out the pieces as thinly as possible without tearing them. Using a sharp knife, pizza cutter, or cookie or biscuit cutters in a shape you like, cut the dough into 3-by-1-in [7.5-by-2.5-cm] rectangles, 2-in [5-cm] squares or circles, or another shape.

Transfer the crackers to one of the prepared baking sheets, leaving at least ½ in [12 mm] of space between them. Continue rolling the dough pieces and forming more crackers. Once the baking sheets are filled, brush each cracker generously on both sides with olive oil. Sprinkle the top sides generously with flaky sea salt.

Bake, rotating the pans halfway through baking, until the crackers are golden brown and the dough has bubbled in places, 10 to 12 minutes. Remove and let cool slightly on the sheet, then transfer the crackers to a drying rack and let cool completely. Store in an airtight container for up to 2 weeks.

GRILLED CROSTINI

The word "crostino" may refer to an appetizer of something—such as a vegetable or some meat, fish, beans, fruit, or cheese—eaten atop toasted bread. In Italian culture, it also refers to the piece of toasted bread itself. Crostini (plural of crostino) are wonderful prepared on a grill pan where they can pick up a little char while they crisp, but a regular skillet or 400°F [200°C] oven works well for toasting them, too. Apply olive oil sparingly so as not to oversoak the center of the bread. If using the oven, bake for 6 to 10 minutes, or until the bread is crisped and browned to your liking.

Twelve ¼-in [6-mm] slices baguette or country-style bread, sliced on a long diagonal

Extra-virgin olive oil, for brushing

Kosher salt

MAKES 12

See photo page 76

Preheat a grill pan or grill over medium-high heat.

Meanwhile, brush each piece of bread on both sides with a moderate amount of olive oil and season lightly with salt. Grill the bread slices in a single layer, turning with tongs as needed, until lightly charred on both sides and crispy, 7 to 8 minutes total.

Carta di Musica (page 35)

Taralli (page 42)

Grissini (page 44)

Olive Oil and Sea Salt Crackers
with Whole Wheat (page 38)

TARALLI

These dry, crumbly, ring-shaped biscuits are abundant in southern Italy, especially Puglia, where they originated. They are one of my favorite snacks on earth, addictive on their own, but also delicious alongside a charcuterie or cheese plate or other antipasti assortment. Baking them atop a drying rack helps ensure an even browning and drying all around—the key to their satisfying crunch—but if you don't have one, gently pat the *taralli* dry on a clean kitchen towel and bake them on a parchment paper–lined baking sheet. Fennel seed is a classic seasoning, but you can replace it with 1¼ tsp of coarsely ground black pepper, if desired, or leave the dough plain.

2 cups [260 g] unbleached all-purpose flour

1 cup [143 g] bread flour

2¼ tsp kosher salt, plus more for simmering

1½ tsp fennel seeds, toasted and cooled (optional)

1 cup [240 ml] dry white wine

½ cup [120 ml] plus 2 Tbsp extra-virgin olive oil

MAKES ABOUT 48

See photo page 40

Place a large drying rack inside a large rimmed baking sheet and set aside.

In a medium bowl, combine the flours, 2¼ tsp salt, and the fennel seeds (if using) and stir briefly with a fork to combine. Add the wine and olive oil and mix with a fork until a crumbly dough begins to form.

Turn out the dough onto a clean work surface and knead into a ball (it will be dry). Continue kneading until the dough feels moist and springy, about 5 minutes. Drape the dough with a towel and set it in a bowl to rest for 30 minutes.

Using a sharp paring knife, cut a very small piece [about ¼ oz, or 7 g] from the dough. Wet your fingertips very lightly in a small bowl of water, then roll the dough piece into a thin snake 3 to 4 in [7.5 to 10 cm] long (the water on your hands will help create a smooth shape; do not overwet the dough as it will prevent the taralli ends from sticking together). Wrap the dough around your index finger and press the ends together to seal, twisting slightly like a twist tie. Transfer to the drying rack and repeat with the remaining dough until you have 12 to 20 taralli.

Meanwhile, fill a medium saucepan with enough water to reach about 5 in [12 cm] up the sides of the pot. Bring to a simmer over medium-high heat, then season generously with salt; bring the water back to a simmer. Add the prepared taralli and cook until they naturally float to the top, 2 to 3 minutes, checking that they're not sticking to the bottom of the pot.

With a slotted spoon, carefully remove and transfer to the drying rack atop the baking sheet (you can place the taralli relatively close together; just check that the prettier sides face up). Let dry while you repeat forming and simmering the remaining taralli.

Preheat the oven to 400°F [200°C].

Dry any remaining water on the baking sheet and bake (the rack should be set in the baking sheet and the taralli should be atop the rack) until golden, 30 to 35 minutes.

Remove and let cool completely. The taralli will dry and crisp further while cooling. Store in an airtight container for up to 1 month.

Flavoring Homemade Taralli

Though amply flavorful on their own, you can season these taralli with any combination of spices, seeds, or herbs you like. Mix the ingredients into the flour mixture before combining it with the wet ingredients to make the dough. Some seasonings to try:

Fresh or dried rosemary leaves

Fresh or dried thyme leaves

Fennel seeds

Coarsely ground black pepper

Ground mustard powder or mustard seeds

Grated Parmigiano-Reggiano or Pecorino Romano cheese

Dried garlic powder or flakes

White or black sesame seeds

Poppy seeds

GRISSINI

Originally from Turin, these skinny, crispy bread-sticks appear on the tables of many restaurants all over Italy. Their long length makes them fun to munch through from one end to the next, and they're wonderful for staving off hunger. Preparing them at home makes me absolutely giddy. And at the table they act both as an elegant snack and a centerpiece of sorts.

The first batch from the oven always comes out the most diverse in shape, but the goal is to make them as consistently skinny as possible so they brown evenly and well. The browner they are, the crispier they will be—overly puffy *grissini* won't crisp properly.

1 tsp sugar

1 package [2¼ tsp] active dry yeast

½ cup [65 g] plus 1 Tbsp white whole-wheat flour

1½ cups [195 g] unbleached all-purpose flour, plus more for dusting

Fine sea salt

2 Tbsp extra-virgin olive oil, plus more for greasing the bowl

Sesame seeds, coarse cornmeal, and poppy seeds, for rolling (optional)

MAKES ABOUT 36

See photo page 41

In a small bowl, combine ¾ cup [180 ml] lukewarm water, the sugar, yeast, and 1 Tbsp of white whole-wheat flour. Whisk well and let rest until tiny bubbles start to form, 3 to 5 minutes.

In the bowl of a stand mixer fitted with the paddle attachment, combine the all-purpose flour and remaining ½ cup [65 g] of white whole-wheat flour. Add 1¼ tsp of salt. Whisk to incorporate.

To the bowl with the yeast, whisk in the olive oil.

With the mixer running on low speed, start streaming the liquid mixture into the dry ingredients. Once the dough forms, you may need to hold the mixer bowl in place or switch to the dough hook; continue beating until the dough looks elastic and smooth, 3 to 4 minutes more. Transfer to a work surface lightly dusted with all-purpose flour and form into a neat ball.

Lightly oil a medium bowl and place the dough ball in it. Cover the bowl with plastic wrap and let sit in a warm place until doubled in size, 45 minutes to 1 hour.

Preheat the oven to 375°F [190°C] and line two large baking sheets with parchment paper.

Cut the dough into 4 wedges and wrap 3 under the plastic wrap. With the fourth, working one piece at a time, cut off little pieces of dough and roll them into ⅛-in-[4-mm-] thick snakes (about 9 pieces total). If the grissini are any thicker than this, they won't get super crispy.

Roll the dough in a little more sea salt or a combination of sea salt and either sesame seeds, coarse cornmeal, or poppy seeds (if using). Transfer to one of the prepared sheets. If they're too long for the sheet, curl the ends (beware, the curly parts don't get quite as browned and crispy).

When you have one baking sheet's worth, bake until set and lightly browned, about 13 minutes. Remove the sheet and turn over the breadsticks using your fingers. Continue baking until the grissini are very well browned all over, 2 to 3 minutes more.

Transfer the grissini to a drying rack and let the baking sheet cool. Meanwhile, repeat the process on the other baking sheet. Continue cooling and refilling the sheets until all the grissini are baked. Let the grissini cool slightly, then eat immediately or store in an airtight container for 1 to 2 weeks.

While the rest of the world may be muted, dulled, and hushed during winter, meals can be at their most lusty and extravagant this time of year. It's the season of deeply simmered broths and sauces, sizzling roasts, and the patient, slow coaxing of flavor from everything at the market. Everything is less spontaneous and more deliberate, including the way I conceive of gatherings and what to serve at them—trying to create something comforting and generous without going overboard. The recipes in this chapter are a mix of the delicate (citrus salads, boiled beans, bitter greens) and the rich (fried seafood, doughy treats, and, of course, eggplant Parmigiana). These are some of the most satisfying dishes to cook, serve, and linger over at the table.

WINTER

WINTER CITRUS SALAD

with ligurian walnut sauce

In Liguria, land of basil pesto, a walnut-based sauce called *salsa di noci* or *tocco di noci* is everyone's second-favorite *condimento*. The traditional version is a creamy mixture of ground walnuts, garlic, marjoram, and Parmigiano, plus what seemed to have been a dairy product somewhere between clotted cream and ricotta. Today, many versions of the nut mixture exist. I leave the dairy out of this one, focusing on fresh, bright flavors. But the oily nuts still add a richness in which to blanket the tart, juicy winter citrus. Serve this salad at room temperature.

2 oz [55 g] walnuts, very finely chopped or smashed, some nearly ground

¼ cup [60 ml] extra-virgin olive oil

1 Tbsp finely chopped fresh Italian parsley leaves

1 Tbsp finely grated Parmigiano-Reggiano, plus ¼ tsp more for topping

¼ tsp finely chopped, seeded medium-heat chile, such as jalapeño or Fresno (optional)

Kosher salt

Freshly ground black pepper

2 navel oranges [about 1 lb, or 455 g, total], peeled

2 Cara Cara or blood oranges, or a mix [about 10 oz, or 280 g, total], peeled

2 satsuma mandarins or tangerines [about 6 oz, or 170 g, total], peeled and broken into segments

2 Tbsp fresh lemon juice

Torn oil-packed anchovies, for serving (optional)

SERVES 6 TO 8

In a medium bowl, combine the walnuts, olive oil, parsley, 1 Tbsp of cheese, the chile (if using), and a generous pinch each of salt and pepper. Stir well to combine. Set aside.

Using a very sharp knife, slice the navel and Cara Cara oranges crosswise into ¼-in- [6-mm-] thick slices. Remove any large seeds that show through.

On a large platter, arrange the orange slices haphazardly, overlapping them as needed. Scatter the mandarin segments on top. Spoon the walnut topping over the oranges and mandarins, tucking some underneath. Drizzle with the lemon juice. Sprinkle with the remaining ¼ tsp of cheese, a pinch of salt, and some pepper. Garnish with a few coarsely torn anchovies, if desired.

The Citrus Mix

Serving this dish with varying types of oranges gives it lovely diversity in color and flavor. If you can't find the full range of oranges listed, this salad can easily be made with just one type, or with a mix of oranges and small, ruby red grapefruits.

ROASTED SHALLOTS

with sage cream sauce and pomegranate seeds

While in the summer Italians will toss atop the grill any vegetable they have a glut of—often zucchini, eggplant, or peppers slicked in oil—in colder months, a high-heat oven can work similar magic on fall and winter vegetables. Here, shallots still in their crispy skins roast until softened and bronzed. I drizzle them in a sage cream sauce, and sprinkle with pomegranate seeds, which grow wild in the hills of Tuscany and across southern Italy. But if you're low on accoutrements, eat these on their own with just the salt, pepper, and oil in which they were roasted.

1 lb [455 g] shallots, about 12 medium, skins intact

2 Tbsp extra-virgin olive oil

Kosher salt

Freshly ground black pepper

2 Tbsp half-and-half

1 Tbsp mayonnaise

1 packed Tbsp chopped fresh sage leaves

⅓ cup [about 2 oz, or 55 g] pomegranate seeds

Fresh rosemary leaves, for serving

SERVES 6

Preheat the oven to 425°F [220°C].

Halve each shallot (do not peel), some lengthwise and some crosswise for variation. Transfer to a small baking sheet and drizzle with the olive oil. Season generously with salt and pepper and toss to coat. Be sure to place at least half of the shallots cut-side down in the pan.

Bake until the shallots are tender and deeply browned (nearly charred) in places, 25 to 28 minutes. Remove from the oven and transfer to a platter if desired. Turn any shallots as needed so they're all facing cut-side up.

Meanwhile, in a small bowl combine the half-and-half, mayonnaise, sage, and a pinch each of salt and pepper. Stir well to combine. Drizzle the sauce atop the shallots. Sprinkle the pomegranate seeds and a few rosemary leaves all over the shallots and serve.

Cut some shallots through their stems and others crosswise for a varied look. Swivel them to face upward, and serve them directly on their baking sheet or on a platter. If on the pan, the residual heat will lightly warm the sauce.

STUFFED MUSSELS

with bacon and garlic bread crumbs

Cozze ripieni, or stuffed mussels, are an antipasto served in many parts of Italy and one of my favorite party snacks. Usually they're filled with a bread crumb mixture, seasoned with garlic (and grated cheese when prepared in the south), and topped with good olive oil. Making the bread crumbs yourself gives a crumbly, crunchy texture to the filling, rather than a sandy one that's too compacted, as can happen with store-bought dried bread crumbs. I add some crispy bacon and bacon fat to the mix.

1¼ lb [570 g] small mussels, rinsed and cleaned in cool water, about 3½ dozen

4 Tbsp [60 ml] extra-virgin olive oil, plus more as needed

One 5½-oz [155-g] piece of baguette, about half a baguette, coarsely torn into 1- to 2-in [2.5- to 5-cm] pieces

3 bacon slices [3 oz, or 85 g]

2 Tbsp finely chopped garlic

3 Tbsp finely chopped fresh Italian parsley leaves

¼ tsp kosher salt, plus more as needed

2 Tbsp unsalted butter, cut into small pieces (optional)

MAKES ABOUT 40

Fill a large pot with enough water to reach about ¾ in [2 cm] up the sides of the pot and bring to a boil over high heat. Once boiling, add the mussels and 1 Tbsp of olive oil. Cover the pot with a lid and cook, shaking the pan occasionally, until the mussels open, 4 to 5 minutes. Using a slotted spoon, transfer the mussels to a large bowl. Let rest until cool enough to handle. Discard the juices and any mussels that have not opened.

One by one, pluck the mussels from their shells, reserving the meat, and tear the shells in half. In the cleaner side of each shell, place one whole picked mussel; transfer the shells with the mussels to a large clean baking sheet (discard the remaining shells). At this point, you can store the mussels covered in the refrigerator up to overnight.

When ready to bake, preheat the oven to 425°F [220°C] and set a rack in the top third of the oven.

On a large baking sheet, spread the torn baguette pieces. Bake until lightly crispy, about 8 minutes.

Transfer the bread pieces to a food processor. Pulse until some pieces are very fine and some are still a little chunky (nothing should be bigger than, say, half a pea). You will have about 1⅔ cups [155 g]. Transfer to a medium bowl and set aside.

continued

In a medium or large skillet over medium heat, cook the bacon slices, flipping as needed, until well browned and crispy, 10 to 12 minutes. Transfer to a plate, reserving the bacon fat [2 to 4 Tbsp, or 30 to 60 ml, depending on your bacon] in a small bowl. Add the garlic to the bacon fat.

Let the bacon slices cool slightly, then finely chop them.

To the bread crumbs, add the cooked bacon, garlic and bacon fat mixture, remaining 3 Tbsp of olive oil, the parsley, and ¼ tsp salt. Mix well. Taste and adjust the seasoning as needed.

Using a spoon, fill the mussel shells with the bread crumb mixture, patting it down into the shells as you go.

Break the butter (if using) into small chunks with your fingers and place a small piece atop each mussel (or as many mussels as you'd like). Alternatively, very lightly drizzle the mussels with olive oil. Bake until the tops are browned and crispy, about 15 minutes. Remove and let cool ever so slightly, then serve.

BROILED CARTA DI MUSICA

with parmigiano, coppa, and chiles

Served plain, these semolina flatbreads from Sardinia are delicious alongside almost any antipasto. But they also make a phenomenal base onto which you can bake salty melted cheeses and thinly sliced cured meats. What might look like a lot of cheese melts down into a very thin layer—so, when in doubt, pile more on halfway through baking.

8 pieces [about 6 in, or 15 cm each] baked (or prepared) Carta di Musica (page 35)

1¼ cup (1½ oz, or 40 g) Parmigiano-Reggiano, finely grated on a Microplane, plus more if desired

16 small, thin slices coppa [about 3 oz, or 85 g, total], or any salumi you like

16 slices Pickled Chiles (page 25), or fresh chile slices, such as Fresno or jalapeño (optional)

Freshly ground black pepper

SERVES 8

See photo page 36

Preheat the broiler to its highest heat and set a rack in the oven's top shelf.

Line a large baking sheet with aluminum foil and place the prepared carta di musica on top. Distribute half the cheese all over the crackers. Add the coppa slices, scrunching them up in various spots on the crackers, and the chile slices, if using. Top with the remaining cheese and a dusting of black pepper.

Broil until the cheese is fully melted and lightly browned on the edges, 2 to 3 minutes, adding more cheese halfway through the broiling process, if desired. Serve immediately.

ROASTED SARDINES

with red onion and celery agrodolce

Sardines are widely believed to have been named after Sardinia, the southern Italian island where they have historically made up a large part of the local diet. They are still found in abundance there and eaten in other parts of southern Italy including Sicily, commonly either breaded and fried, served in pastas, or stuffed and rolled up as antipasti. You'll often find sardines served with something sweet, like golden raisins or another dried fruit. Here, I top them with sweet-and-sour onion *agrodolce*, with little pieces of celery for crunch.

6 whole sardines [14 oz, or 400 g, total], gutted by your fishmonger

¼ tsp kosher salt, plus more as needed

2 Tbsp dried bread crumbs

Finely grated zest of ¼ lemon

1 Tbsp finely chopped fresh Italian parsley leaves

3 Tbsp extra-virgin olive oil

Freshly ground black pepper

½ large red onion [5 oz, or 140 g], thinly sliced

⅓ cup [80 ml] red wine vinegar

1¼ tsp sugar

1 tsp finely chopped fresh garlic

2 Tbsp sliced celery, from 1 medium inner stalk, leaves reserved

8 pitted olives [¾ oz, or 20 g], such as black, oil-cured, Kalamata, or a mix, halved

Lemon wedges, for serving

SERVES 6

See photo page 2–3

Preheat the oven to 425°F [220°C] and set a rack in the top third.

Gently open and debone the fish (see Sidebar). Rinse inside and out with cool water. Pat dry. Season lightly with ⅛ tsp of salt.

In a small baking dish, line up the sardines. In a small bowl combine the bread crumbs, ⅛ tsp salt, the zest, and parsley. Add 1 Tbsp of olive oil. Spread the mixture atop the sardines. Drizzle with an additional 1 Tbsp of oil and season with pepper. Roast until the bread crumbs are well browned, 26 to 28 minutes.

Meanwhile, in a small skillet over medium-high heat, heat the remaining 1 Tbsp of oil until shimmering. Add the onion and a pinch of salt. Cook, stirring frequently, until softened, 3 minutes. Add the vinegar and sugar and cook, stirring, until most of the liquid evaporates and the onion looks glossy, 3 minutes. Remove from the heat. Stir in the garlic, celery, and olives.

Remove the sardines. Let cool slightly. Top with the onion mixture and the reserved celery leaves. Serve with lemon wedges.

How to Remove Sardine Bones

Holding the belly of the fish open where it's been gutted, grab the spine of the fish near the neck. Pinch and bend to crack the bones loose at the neck, then pull the spine away from the body in one piece. Rinse with cool water to clear away any lingering bones.

GARLIC KNOTS

with fresh parsley

This recipe makes soft, doughy knots with a little crunch around the edges, but the texture largely comes down to the pizza dough you buy. When in doubt, buy dough from a pizza restaurant you like and, in this case, that you know makes soft and chewy pies. I like to drag friends into the kitchen to each fill and roll one of their own knots. Seeing how everyone's turns out makes for a good laugh. Or maybe my friends and I just drink too much.

1½ lb [680 g] good-quality pizza dough

Extra-virgin olive oil, for brushing

3 Tbsp minced fresh garlic

3 Tbsp minced fresh Italian parsley leaves

Kosher salt

All-purpose flour, for dusting

4 Tbsp [56 g] unsalted butter

Garlic powder, for seasoning

Grated Parmigiano-Reggiano, for sprinkling

MAKES 10

Working on a clean counter (do not flour the counter), cut the ball of pizza dough in half. Cut each half into five equal pieces (you'll have ten pieces total).

Stretching gently with your fingers and using a rolling pin to help flatten and stretch the piece, smooth out a dough piece against the counter into about a 10-by-2-in [25-by-5-cm] strip. Brush the inside center lightly with olive oil. Add ¾ tsp of minced garlic, ¾ tsp of minced parsley, and a pinch of salt, rubbing the ingredients up and down the dough piece to spread them evenly. Roll up the dough piece lengthwise like a long worm to cover the filling (the dough pieces will be long and only about ¾ in, or 2 cm, thick at this point). Form a haphazard knot by twisting and tying the piece as you like (see Sidebar, page 58). These do not need to be consistent shapes—have fun.

Transfer to a lightly floured baking sheet and repeat with the remaining dough pieces, garlic, parsley, and salt. (You will have a little garlic and parsley left over; reserve it.)

In a small saucepan over medium heat, melt the butter with the remaining 1½ tsp of minced garlic. Keep warm on the stove's lowest setting.

Preheat the oven to 425°F [220°C].

continued

In the time it takes for the oven to preheat, the dough knots should plump up a little on the sheet. When the oven is hot, brush the knots generously all over the top and sides with some of the garlic butter. Reserve the remaining garlic butter, keeping it warm, for later. Sprinkle each of the knots lightly all over with garlic powder.

Bake until the bottoms are browned, the tops are lightly golden, and the dough is still relatively soft inside, about 20 minutes.

Remove and brush once more with the garlic butter. Sprinkle with the remaining 1½ tsp of minced parsley and a little grated Parmigiano. Serve warm.

My Preferred Knot Method

Using your nondominant hand, hold the tip of a filled dough piece between your thumb and pointer finger, letting the longest part of the dough and the other end drape over the back (top) of your hand. Tightly pull the long end of the dough with your dominant hand and wrap it around your pointer and middle finger twice. Finally pull the end of the dough between the two loops, forming a knot that has two layers of dough.

CHICKEN LIVER CROSTINI

with shallots and butter

It's a word that can make you feel like a true Italian: *fegatini!* And a food that can, too—chicken livers, the pungent, iron-y little nuggets you can find at any Italian meat counter, especially in Tuscany where they're considered the highest quality. Blending the cooked livers with plenty of good butter, a little booze, and some shallots turns them into a smooth, balanced pâté. When classically served slathered upon toasted bread, the combination is called "the most traditional of all crostini" by Italian food writer Anna Del Conte.

1½ lb [680 g] chicken livers, trimmed of any dark spots

Milk, for soaking (optional)

10 Tbsp [140 g] unsalted butter, cut into small cubes

3 Tbsp finely chopped shallot

¾ tsp kosher salt

⅛ tsp freshly ground black pepper

¼ cup [60 ml] cognac, Vin Santo, or any brandy

Grilled Crostini (page 39), for serving

Pickled Red Onions (page 26) or fresh sliced radishes, for serving (optional)

SERVES 8 TO 10

In a medium bowl, combine the livers and just enough milk to cover (if using). Refrigerate until ready to use, up to a few hours. Drain well. This step is optional, but helps clean the livers and subdue any bitter flavors.

Set a strainer in a medium bowl and place it next to the stove. In a large skillet over medium-high heat, melt 2 Tbsp of butter. Once hot, add the shallot. Cook, stirring frequently, until softened, 2 minutes. Add the livers and raise the heat to high. Season with the salt and pepper and cook, stirring occasionally, until brown on the outsides and slightly pink in the center, 3 to 4 minutes total.

Transfer the liver and shallot mixture to the strainer and place the skillet back on the burner. Lower the heat to medium-high and quickly add the cognac to the skillet (stand back, it may sizzle). Cook, stirring, until the cognac is reduced to about 1 Tbsp, about 1 minute. Turn off the heat.

In a food processor, combine the liver and shallot mixture (discard any juices), the cognac mixture, and the remaining 8 Tbsp [112 g] of butter. Process the pâté until smooth.

Using a spatula, transfer the pâté to one or more serving jars (the mixture will be loose). Cover with plastic wrap, pressing the wrap against the surface of the pâté, to prevent a film from forming. Chill until set, 1 to 2 hours. The pâté can be stored in the refrigerator overnight at this point.

When ready to serve, make the crostini (page 39). Let cool slightly. Spread each with a thin to moderate layer of pâté and garnish with pickled onions, if desired. Serve immediately.

WINTER LETTUCES

with bagna cauda

Bagna cauda is a warm anchovy- and garlic-based dressing from Italy's Piemonte area. It's typically served with raw vegetables, like asparagus, carrots, or artichokes, for dipping. I also enjoy it drizzled atop the bitter lettuces that come out during winter, with their pretty frizzled leaves and speckled colors. I've stubbornly tried it before using only olive oil, but the butter is essential to rounding out its flavor and texture.

6 oz [170 g] bitter winter lettuce or chicory leaves, ideally Italian, such as Rosa di Gorizia or radicchio di Castelfranco, rinsed and dried

½ cup [120 ml] extra-virgin olive oil

12 oil-packed anchovy fillets [about 2 oz, or 55 g, total], finely chopped

6 medium garlic cloves [½ oz, or 15 g], minced

4 Tbsp [56 g] unsalted butter, cut into cubes

Freshly ground black pepper

Juice of ½ lemon

SERVES 6

Arrange the leaves in a pleasing way atop a platter and refrigerate them briefly.

In a saucepan over medium-low heat, combine the olive oil, anchovies, and garlic. Cook, whisking frequently, until the anchovies break up fully into the oil and the garlic no longer tastes sharp, 12 to 14 minutes. Add the butter and let melt, whisking constantly to combine and emulsify. Season with pepper, taste, and adjust the seasoning as needed. It is important to serve bagna cauda while it's still warm and emulsified.

Retrieve the lettuces. Whisk the bagna cauda a final time and spoon some of the dressing atop the leaves. Drizzle lightly with lemon juice and serve immediately.

BAKED SQUASH

with chili oil and crispy seeds

Gourds have been eaten in Italy since Roman times. Some say the large ones were used as wine vessels at feasts. Beautiful, sometimes warty, and firm-skinned cold-weather varietals in the country include the beautifully named northern *marina di Chioggia*, southern *zucca piena di Napoli*, and, of course, the pumpkin—the star of Emilia's winter tortelli. I chose to work with a newer squash variety called the carnival squash, a relative of an acorn squash, with striated, speckled sides and a nutty-tasting orange flesh. I steam-roast the pieces, sprinkle them with their own toasted seeds, and smear them with crème fraîche and chili oil. You can roast the squash ahead and drape it with aluminum foil until antipasto time. I love to serve the thick wedges atop a broad, flat platter or clean, decorative baking sheet or tray.

Dried Chili Oil (page 30), for serving

2 medium carnival squash or acorn squash [3½ lb, or 1.6 kg total]

6 garlic cloves, in their skins

3 Tbsp extra-virgin olive oil

¼ tsp kosher salt

Crème fraîche or full-fat Greek yogurt, for serving

Freshly ground black pepper

SERVES 8

Be sure your chili oil is prepared and cooling.

Preheat the oven to 425°F [220°C].

Halve the squash with a long, sharp knife and spoon out the center, reserving the seeds. Cut each squash half lengthwise into 2 or 3 wedges.

On a large rimmed baking sheet, add the squash and garlic. Drizzle with the olive oil and sprinkle with the salt. Rub to coat the squash pieces all over. Position each squash wedge with one cut edge against the pan. Add ⅓ cup [80 ml] of water to the pan and cover the pan tightly with aluminum foil. Roast until the water evaporates, about 30 minutes. Remove from the oven.

Meanwhile, rinse the reserved seeds in a strainer while pulling away and discarding any remaining pieces of squash. (If the seeds aren't *completely* clean, that's okay.) Drain.

Remove and discard the aluminum foil from the baking sheet and add the cleaned squash seeds to the pan, scattering them all over the surface. Continue roasting until the squash pieces are browned in places and the seeds are browned and crispy, 25 to 30 minutes more.

Transfer the squash pieces and garlic cloves to a platter (peel the garlic cloves, if desired). Smear or dollop each of the squash pieces with a little crème fraîche. Drizzle the squash with chili oil and sprinkle with the toasted seeds and black pepper. Serve.

BLACK LENTILS

with burrata and baby spinach

Burrata is a crowd-pleaser, but I like to serve it with something that adds texture, color, and a little relief from all its intense creaminess. Lentils are beloved in many parts of Italy—some brown, some tiny and emerald green, but I use the deep, shiny black kind here, which are some of the fastest to cook and keep their texture better than other varieties. I mix them with gently cooked red onions and spinach to form a little nest for the burrata. Have bread or Grilled Crostini (page 39) handy for mopping up any remnants of burrata in the bowl.

One 8-oz [230-g] burrata ball

½ cup black lentils [3¼ oz, or 90 g], rinsed well

Kosher salt

2 Tbsp extra-virgin olive oil

½ medium red onion [4 oz, or 115 g], halved, then thinly sliced

Freshly ground black pepper

1 Tbsp red wine vinegar

3 packed cups [about 4½ oz, or 130 g] fresh baby spinach leaves

Lemon wedges, for squeezing (optional)

SERVES 4 TO 6

Remove the burrata from the refrigerator and let it come to room temperature.

Meanwhile, in a small saucepan, combine the lentils with enough water to cover by 1 in [2.5 cm]. Season with a pinch of salt and bring to a strong simmer over high heat. Cook until the lentils are tender but not yet mushy or split, 12 to 14 minutes. Strain.

In a large nonstick skillet over medium-high heat, heat 1 Tbsp of olive oil. Add the red onion and season with a pinch of salt and pepper. Cook, stirring occasionally, until softened slightly, 1 to 2 minutes. Stir in the vinegar and cook, stirring frequently, until most of the vinegar evaporates, about 2 minutes. Add the spinach and season lightly with salt and pepper. Cook, stirring constantly, until most pieces are just wilted, about 3 minutes. Add the strained lentils and stir gently to combine. Taste and adjust the seasoning as needed.

Transfer the lentil mixture to a shallow serving bowl or rimmed plate in a thin layer. Place the burrata in the center. Drizzle with the remaining 1 Tbsp of olive oil and sprinkle with salt and pepper. Serve with lemon wedges for squeezing, if desired.

ROASTED VEGETABLE PLATTER

with fennel tzatziki

This throng of roasted vegetables is the cold-weather answer to spring's raw crudités platter. Everything cooks together in the oven for ease, but if one vegetable is taking particularly long to tenderize, just cook it a little longer and remove the others to the platter.

My twist to slightly "Italianize" tzatziki sauce—the cooling Greek cucumber-yogurt dip—is to use fennel fronds in place of the traditional chopped dill.

VEGETABLE PLATTER

1 lb [455 g] baby beets, about 8 small, a mix of golden, red, or Chioggia, peeled, green stems trimmed to about 1 in [2.5 cm]

5 medium slender carrots [about 12 oz, or 340 g, total], any color, scrubbed well, thicker ones halved lengthwise, green stems trimmed to about 1 in [2.5 cm]

1 medium [about 12-oz, or 340-g] celery root, peeled, halved, and sliced into ½-in- [12-mm-] thick wedges

1 medium [12-oz, or 340-g] fennel bulb with fronds, stalks trimmed, bulb sliced into ½-in- [12-mm-] thick wedges, fronds reserved for the dip (see following)

6 small parsnips [about 9 oz, or 255 g, total], scrubbed well, thicker ones halved lengthwise

1 medium [about 8-oz, or 230-g] red onion, peeled and sliced through the root into ¾-in- [2-cm-] thick wedges

4 Tbsp [60 ml] extra-virgin olive oil

Kosher salt

Coarsely ground black pepper

Few fresh sprigs winter herbs, such as thyme and rosemary, coarsely torn, for garnishing

FENNEL TZATZIKI

1 cup [240 g] whole-milk Greek yogurt

1 medium [about 5-oz, or 140-g] seedless cucumber or one 5-oz [140-g] piece English cucumber, grated on the fine side of a box grater [5 Tbsp, or 75 ml, total of flesh and juice], or more as needed

1 Tbsp plus 2 tsp fresh lemon juice, from about 1 large lemon, or more as needed

2 tsp coarsely torn or chopped fennel fronds

½ tsp finely grated fresh garlic

¼ tsp kosher salt

⅛ tsp freshly ground black pepper

SERVES 8 TO 10

MAKE THE VEGETABLE PLATTER: Preheat the oven to 450°F [230°C]. Set one rack nearest the oven's heat source and the other in the next closest position.

On two large rimmed baking sheets, place the vegetables in individual piles, keeping like ones grouped together. Drizzle the vegetables on each baking sheet with 2 Tbsp of olive oil and sprinkle each evenly with ¼ tsp plus ⅛ tsp salt and a generous amount of pepper. Toss each pile to coat the vegetables fully, keeping the piles separate. Spread the vegetables into a single layer on each baking sheet, leaving as much room as possible between the pieces.

continued

Roast until the vegetables are lightly browned on one side, about 25 minutes. Flip or toss most of the vegetables, and rotate the pans on the racks. Continue roasting until the vegetables are well browned and mostly tender with a slight bite, about 10 minutes more. Remove and let cool slightly.

MEANWHILE, MAKE THE FENNEL TZATZIKI: In a medium serving bowl, combine the yogurt, cucumber and its juices, lemon juice, fennel fronds, garlic, salt, and pepper. Stir well. Taste and adjust the seasoning and consistency, as desired, adding more lemon juice or cucumber juice to thin the yogurt if needed.

On an extra-large platter, arrange the vegetables in piles around the edges. Sprinkle them decoratively with the coarsely torn herb sprigs, or more salt and pepper, if desired. Serve the vegetables either warm or at room temperature, with the prepared dip.

Styling a Vegetable Platter

To me, arranging a vegetable platter in a beautiful way is half the fun of serving it. Here's what to keep in mind:

It's just a vegetable platter. It will taste delicious no matter how it looks!

For a more unified look, cut all the vegetables into similar sizes before arranging them.

Separate like colors from one another to create color contrast around the platter. I do this by arranging a pile of dark-colored vegetables next to a pile of light ones, and so on, letting this continue around the board or platter.

Let some long or pointed vegetables or the frayed edges of others dangle outside the edges of the platter to give a more interesting shape to the dish.

Place like vegetables in varying directions (for example, pointing the carrots haphazardly instead of lining them up in a row) for a messy but artful look.

Garnish with pretty sprigs of herbs or large spices like star anise, bay leaves, or strips of orange zest. They won't really add any flavor but they will add an extra visual layer and help decorate (and hide imperfections of) the platter.

Play around with placing the dip slightly off-center on the plate, then tuck the vegetables around it as they fit.

EGGPLANT PARMIGIANA

The Italians sometimes serve little squares of eggplant Parmigiana before the first course, often close to room temperature. It's also a filling dish that, in larger slices, can sustain people easily as a main course. My relatives in Calabria add a layer each of prosciutto slices and sliced hard-boiled egg into theirs before baking it—something to try if you're feeling ambitious.

SAUCE

2 large [28-oz, or 800-g] cans plum tomatoes

3 Tbsp extra-virgin olive oil

6 large garlic cloves, peeled

Kosher salt

Freshly ground black pepper

EGGPLANT

3 large eggs

Kosher salt

1¼ cups [175 g] dried plain fine bread crumbs

1 Tbsp dried Italian seasoning or equal parts dried basil, dried rosemary, and dried oregano

3 medium eggplants [about 3 lb, or 1.35 kg, total], mostly peeled except for a few strips of skin, sliced into thin rounds slightly thinner than ¼ in [6 mm]

About 1 cup [240 ml] olive oil

1½ cups [about 10½ oz, or 300 g] shredded mozzarella cheese (not fresh)

3 Tbsp finely grated Pecorino Romano

MAKES ONE 9-BY-13-IN
[23-BY-33-CM] PAN; SERVES 8 TO 12

MAKE THE SAUCE: In a blender, pulse the tomatoes and their juices until just slightly chunky.

In a medium-large [4-quart, or 3.8-L, or so] heavy-bottomed pot over medium-low heat, heat the olive oil and garlic, stirring occasionally, until the garlic is softened slightly and fragrant but not yet browned, about 4 minutes. Pour in the puréed tomato mixture all at once and season with a generous pinch each of salt and pepper. Bring to a gentle simmer and cook, stirring frequently from the bottom of the pot, until thickened slightly, at least 1 to 1½ hours.

If you're baking and serving right away, preheat the oven to 400°F [200°C] and place an oven rack in the top part of the oven. If not, skip the preheat for now.

BREAD THE EGGPLANT: In a medium baking dish or wide shallow bowl, beat the eggs with 1 Tbsp of water. Season with a generous pinch of salt. In a second baking dish or bowl, stir together the bread crumbs, ½ tsp of salt, and the Italian seasoning.

One or two at a time, dredge the eggplant slices in the egg wash and let the excess drip back into the bowl. Transfer to the bread crumbs and coat very lightly on each side.

continued

Line a large baking sheet with a few layers of paper towels and set it next to the stove. In a large high-sided skillet over medium-high heat, heat ½ cup [120 ml] of olive oil until shimmering. Turn the heat to medium and add some eggplant rounds in a single layer until the pan is full. Cook, turning once, until the slices are well browned on each side, about 6 minutes total. Transfer to the prepared baking sheet. Repeat with the remaining eggplant slices, working in batches as needed and adding a little more oil every other batch, or as needed. As you work, continue to add layers of paper towels between the eggplant pieces so they remain separate.

If you're not serving the eggplant right away, refrigerate the pieces in a sealed container for up to 1 day. Let the sauce cool and refrigerate it separately for up to 2 days. If serving right away, set a 9-by-13-in [23-by-33-cm] baking dish on the counter.

Start by ladling ½ cup [120 ml] plus 2 Tbsp of sauce into the bottom of the dish. Cover the sauce with a single layer of eggplant (start with the thickest ones on the bottom, and save the prettiest slices for the top). Ladle another ½ cup [120 ml] of sauce over, spreading it evenly. Sprinkle with 1 Tbsp of grated romano and about ⅓ cup [66 g] plus 2 Tbsp of mozzarella. Add another layer of eggplant and repeat this process until you've reached the final layer of eggplant. Top this layer only with ½ cup [120 ml] of sauce, a final thin layer of mozzarella, and some grated romano. (You will likely have a little leftover sauce.)

At this point, you can cover the baking dish with plastic wrap and refrigerate up to 1 day.

Bake the eggplant Parmigiana uncovered in the top part of the oven until the cheese is melted and bronzed in places and the sauce is bubbling around the edges, about 20 minutes (add about 10 minutes if your dish was previously assembled and chilled). Remove and let cool slightly. Slice into squares and serve warm.

Timing Eggplant Parm

A portion this size can take about 3 hours, start to finish, to make, and it's best done with a partner. But you can break up the steps by cooking the sauce up to a few days ahead and frying the eggplant slices a few hours, or up to a day, before. If you do chill the assembled eggplant Parmigiana before baking it, add a few extra minutes to the baking time.

CRISPY PORK RIBS

with scallion-ginger herb sauce

I've always liked the idea of wintry preparations for ribs—why should we have to wait until summer to enjoy them? In traditional Italian recipes, you find ribs roasted or stewed and then nestled into thick soups or pastas. But in this more American preparation, slow cooking them in the oven and then smearing them with sauce before broiling creates soft meat with crispy edges. They make a fun, finger-friendly antipasto or main.

RIBS

2 racks baby back pork ribs [about 4 lb 10 oz, or 2.1 kg, total], membranes removed

4 tsp kosher salt

Freshly ground black pepper

1 small head garlic, top sliced off

SCALLION-GINGER HERB SAUCE

½ cup [120 ml] plus 1 Tbsp extra-virgin olive oil

½ cup [50 g] coarsely chopped peeled fresh ginger

2 bunches scallions [1⅓ cups, or 185 g], trimmed and thinly sliced

1 packed cup [40 g] coarsely chopped fresh Italian parsley leaves

1½ tsp soy sauce

½ tsp white wine vinegar

¼ tsp sugar

¼ tsp kosher salt

Freshly ground black pepper

SERVES 8

Preheat the oven to 325°F [165°C].

MAKE THE RIBS: Season the ribs with salt and pepper and wrap each rib rack tightly in two layers of sturdy aluminum foil. Wrap the garlic in a separate pouch of foil. Place the ribs and garlic together on a large baking sheet. Roast for 1 hour, 45 minutes, at which point the meat should shred easily and feel tender when poked with a paring knife. Remove and let cool slightly. Remove the garlic from its foil pack and squeeze the cloves out of their skins; transfer to a small food processor.

Preheat the broiler to its highest setting and position a rack in the top position.

MEANWHILE, MAKE THE SCALLION-GINGER HERB SAUCE: To the roasted garlic in the food processor, add the olive oil and ginger. Pulse until finely ground. Add 1 cup [140 g] of scallions, the parsley, soy sauce, vinegar, sugar, salt, and pepper. Pulse until a chunky paste forms. Stir in the remaining ⅓ cup [45 g] of scallions.

Unwrap the ribs and brush the top side of each rack generously with some of the herb sauce (carefully transfer the pork juices to a bowl, let cool, and discard). Place the ribs under the broiler in the top rack and broil until deeply browned, about 10 minutes. Remove, cut between the ribs, and brush each with a little more sauce. Serve with extra sauce on the side.

STEWED CALAMARI

with tomato, capers, and collard greens

This is a magnificent dish for a winter gathering—from the warming quality it lends, fortified with a little vodka and a lot of hearty greens, to its festive colors. It's ready as soon as the squid tastes tender, at which point you can put out the pot with a stack of spoons and bowls. People will flock to it, wherever it lands.

2 Tbsp extra-virgin olive oil, plus more for brushing the bread

1 cup [4¼ oz, or 120 g] chopped onion, from ½ large white onion

Kosher salt

Freshly ground black pepper

4 medium garlic cloves [about 1 Tbsp], finely chopped

1 Tbsp vodka (optional)

1¾ cups [427 g] canned crushed plum tomatoes and their juices

5 sprigs fresh thyme

1 Tbsp plus 1 tsp drained capers in brine

Chili flakes, for seasoning

1 lb [455 g] calamari, tubes thinly sliced into rings, tentacles halved if large

⅓ cup [40 g] finely chopped celery and celery leaves, from about 1 large stalk

8 slices hearty bread, cut on a diagonal, or Grilled Crostini (page 39), for serving

1½ cups [about 1½ oz, or 40 g] chopped collard greens

SERVES 6 TO 8

Preheat the oven to 400°F [200°C]. Alternatively, if making Grilled Crostini (page 39), take out the grill pan.

Meanwhile, in a large Dutch oven or pot over medium-high heat, heat the olive oil until shimmering. Add the onion. Season with ¼ tsp salt and a pinch of pepper. Cook, stirring occasionally, until softened and lightly browned in places, about 4 minutes. Add the garlic and lower the heat to medium. Cook, stirring occasionally, for 1 minute more. Pour in the vodka (if using) and stir in the tomatoes, thyme, capers, and a pinch of chili flakes. Bring the mixture to a simmer. Add the calamari and celery and adjust the heat to maintain a simmer. Cook until the calamari has shrunken slightly and tastes tender, about 30 minutes.

On a baking sheet, place the bread slices in a single layer and brush lightly with olive oil. Bake until crispy and browned, 6 to 10 minutes or grill on a grill pan over medium-high heat, turning as needed for 7 to 8 minutes. Remove from the oven.

Stir the collard greens into the calamari mixture. Cook, stirring occasionally, until wilted, 2 to 3 minutes. Transfer to a serving bowl and serve with the toasts and individual bowls for eating.

THINLY SLICED TUSCAN PORK LOIN

with rosemary, sage, and anchovy

There are only a few truly memorable roast meats that come to mind when I think of my travels around Italy. But one that won my heart is a Tuscan or Florentine-style roast pork—*arista alla fiorentina*—which is often served just slightly warm, usually with white beans. Rosemary and garlic are common seasonings, but the anchovy gives the roast that special something—saltiness and savoriness, without any noticeably fishy flavors. I sear the meat early, then finish with a slow, low-heat method so I can have it well on its way (and have the kitchen clean) before friends arrive. This low-heat method also helps the loin stay moist and tender.

4 large garlic cloves, peeled

2 Tbsp fresh rosemary leaves

2 Tbsp chopped fresh sage leaves

1 oil-packed anchovy fillet (optional)

5 Tbsp [75 ml] extra-virgin olive oil

2 lb [910 g] boneless center-cut pork loin (not tenderloin), tied tightly crosswise about every 2 in [5 cm] with butcher twine

About ¾ tsp kosher salt

SERVES 6

Preheat the oven to 225°F [110°C] and position a rack in the center of the oven.

Meanwhile, in the bowl of a small food processor, combine the garlic, rosemary, sage, anchovy (if using), and 3 Tbsp of olive oil. Grind to a coarse paste and set aside.

Season the meat all over with the salt, rubbing the meat to coat it.

In a large ovenproof skillet over medium-high heat, heat the remaining 2 Tbsp of olive oil until shimmering. Add the pork loin (the meat should sizzle vigorously when it hits the pan). Cook, rotating the meat two or three times, until deep golden brown on all sides, 8 to 10 minutes total. Turn off the heat but leave the meat in the pan. With an offset spatula or pastry brush, coat the meat with most of the herb mixture (reserve about 1 Tbsp for brushing on the meat later).

Transfer the pan to the center rack in the oven and bake until the meat is tender and moist, 2 hours to 2 hours, 20 minutes. A thermometer inserted into the center of the meat may read about 180°F [82°C], but don't worry, the meat is not overcooked and will still be juicy.

Remove from the oven and brush the top and sides of the meat with the reserved 1 Tbsp of the herb mixture. Let the meat cool for 3 to 5 minutes. Transfer to a cutting board but reserve the juices and fat from the pan. Slice the meat very thinly [about ⅛ in, or 4 mm], and arrange the slices on a serving platter. Drizzle with the juices and herbs from the bottom of the pan. Serve warm or at room temperature.

LANGOUSTINES AND CLAMS

in fennel broth with chiles

The clickety-clack of working with shellfish is a special music I love in the kitchen. Each type has its own tone—here, it's the pebble-like *click clock* of little cockles clanking together, and the high-pitched squeaks of langoustine shells being scrubbed under running water. After cooking them both in a quick, lightly sweet fennel broth, eating them is a hands-on affair, which can transport you to the likes of a summer clam feast or crawfish boil even in winter. I don't know anyone who wouldn't dive right into this dish.

If langoustines prove hard to find at the fish market, use shell-on shrimp or cooked crab legs broken into manageable segments.

1 lb [455 g] cockles or other small clams

6 large langoustines [1¼ lb, or 570 g, total], scrubbed clean

2 Tbsp extra-virgin olive oil

½ white onion, halved and thinly sliced

1 large [12-oz, or 340-g] fennel bulb, trimmed, quartered lengthwise, then thinly sliced, plus fennel fronds, for garnishing

½ cup [120 ml] dry white wine

1¼ cups [300 ml] low-sodium chicken broth

2 garlic cloves, thinly sliced

2 Tbsp chopped fresh chives

1 long red chile, thinly sliced

Crusty bread, for serving

SERVES 4

Purge the clams (see Sidebar, page 103). Drain and set aside.

Meanwhile, prepare the langoustines by holding their backs down against a cutting board and cutting a long slit down the inner sides of their tails (do not cut all the way through). This will make the meat easier to pick out later.

In a large [6-qt, or 5.7-L] Dutch oven or heavy-bottomed pot over medium-high heat, heat the olive oil. Add the onion and cook, stirring, until softened slightly, 2 minutes. Add the fennel and cook, stirring occasionally, until slightly softened, 2 to 3 minutes. Pour in the wine and the broth. Raise the heat to high and bring the mixture to a simmer. Lower the heat as needed to maintain a simmer. Add the langoustines and cover the pot. Cook until the shells are bright orange (the meat should be just cooked through), about 6 minutes. Add the garlic and clams to the langoustine mixture, stirring to incorporate, and cover the pot. Simmer until the clams open, 2 to 3 minutes.

Uncover the pot and discard any clams that do not open. Transfer the seafood and broth to a serving bowl if desired. Garnish with the chopped chives and some sliced chile and fennel fronds. Serve immediately with crusty bread.

ROASTED ROMANESCO AND CAULIFLOWER

with black oil-cured olives

Romanesco, which today Americans have shortened in name from the formal *broccolo romano* or *broccolo romanesco*, was once cultivated only near Rome. It tastes like a cross between broccoli and cauliflower, but cooks most similarly to cauliflower, which is why you can roast both together in the same pan to good success. This preparation is straightforward, letting the crunch and caramelized flavors of the brassicas shine, and adding oil-cured black olives. The olives are dry-brined and then macerated in oil, and have a pronounced flavor and wrinkly, prune-like texture.

4 cups romanesco florets,
from about 1 medium [1-lb-3-oz, or 540-g] head

3 cups cauliflower florets,
from about 1 small [1-lb, or 455-g] head

8 garlic cloves, peeled

¼ cup [60 ml] extra-virgin olive oil

¼ tsp kosher salt

Freshly ground black pepper

¼ cup [40 g] oil-cured black olives

Lemon wedges, for squeezing (optional)

SERVES 8

Preheat the oven to 425°F [220°C].

On a large baking sheet (lined with aluminum foil, if desired), add the romanesco, cauliflower, and garlic. Drizzle with the olive oil and sprinkle with the salt and some pepper. Toss to coat.

Bake until the vegetables are browned in places and al dente throughout, 30 to 35 minutes. Remove from the oven.

Add the olives, taste, and sprinkle with some lemon juice, if desired. Serve from the baking sheet or transfer to a serving bowl.

SHRIMP AND FENNEL FRITTO MISTO

with chili mayo

Fritto misto, literally "mixed fry," traditionally incorporates anything from vegetables to seafood to organ meats beneath its delicate golden batter. You can prepare a sizeable batch in a pot filled about 3 in [7.5 cm] high with frying oil—no deep-fryer required. Like most battered foods, keeping *fritto misto* waiting won't do much for its crunch factor, so be prepared to cook, serve, and eat it right away.

DIPPING SAUCE

1 tsp Spicy Pepper Relish (page 31),
Sriracha or other chili sauce, plus more as desired

⅓ cup [80 g] mayonnaise

FRITTO MISTO

12 large shell-on shrimp [about 12 oz, or 340 g]

1 medium [about 8-oz, or 230-g] fennel bulb, trimmed

½ large lemon

Few small sprigs fresh parsley,
long stems trimmed away

Canola oil, for frying

BATTER

1 cup [240 ml] ice-cold water

½ cup [66 g] cornstarch

½ cup [65 g] sifted all-purpose flour

Kosher salt

SERVES 6

PREPARE THE DIPPING SAUCE: In a small bowl, stir together the chili sauce and mayonnaise.

PREPARE THE FRITTO MISTO: Peel and devein the bodies of the shrimp, but leave the heads and tails on some or all, if desired. Slice the fennel bulb lengthwise into ¾-in- [2-cm-] thick wedges. Finally, slice the lemon half into very thin slices.

Set the prepared shrimp, fennel wedges, lemon slices, and parsley sprigs on a large platter or small baking sheet next to the stove. Set a paper towel–lined platter next to the stove as well.

In a medium or large saucepan, add enough canola oil to reach at least 3 in [7.5 cm] up the sides of the pot. Heat over medium-high heat until the oil's temperature registers 360°F [182°C] on a deep-fat thermometer.

MEANWHILE, PREPARE THE BATTER: Place the ice-cold water in a medium bowl. Add the cornstarch and whisk to combine. Add the flour and stir gently with a fork until mostly incorporated but some chunks remain (do not overmix).

Working with four to five pieces at a time, dredge the prepared ingredients in the batter. Let some of the excess drip off. Transfer to the hot oil and fry, turning as needed, until cooked through and lightly golden, about 2 minutes.

Using a slotted spoon or spider, transfer the cooked ingredients to the prepared plate. Immediately sprinkle with salt. Repeat with the remaining items and batter and serve hot with the chili mayo.

ESCAROLE AND ANCHOVY HAND PIES

with crispy pizza dough

Escarole pies, or *pizza di scarola*, are a Neapolitan tradition, usually served on Christmas Eve, or sometimes New Year's Day. This recipe was passed down to my great-grandmother from her grandmother in Italy. Each hand pie is packed full with fresh escarole leaves, which cook down into a thin layer while the pizza dough fries in the pan. If someone didn't like anchovies, she substituted salty slices of fresh mozzarella in their pie.

These pies freeze incredibly well after they're cooked. Wrap them in aluminum foil or place in a resealable plastic bag, freeze, then bake at 350°F [180°C] until warmed through and crispy.

All-purpose flour, for dusting

1 lb [455 g] pizza dough,
fully risen and at room temperature

1 lb [455 g] rinsed and dried escarole leaves,
coarsely torn [8 packed cups]

24 oil-packed anchovies,
from about one 3⅓-oz [95-g] jar

Extra-virgin olive oil, for frying

MAKES 8

Line a baking sheet with parchment paper and very lightly dust it with all-purpose flour. Set aside.

Cut the pizza dough into 8 even [2-oz, or 55-g] wedges. Form each into a ball. Begin working with the first piece of dough and drape the others with a clean kitchen towel. Stretch the dough, being careful not to create any holes, into as thin a piece as possible (it will be around 5 by 8 in, or 12 by 20 cm). Laying the dough flat on a work surface and starting near one of the shorter edges, pile 1 packed cup [2 oz, or 55 g] of the escarole leaves onto half of the dough, leaving a thin border around the edges. Top the escarole with 3 anchovy fillets, distributing them around the pie. Pick up the remaining clean side of dough and lift and stretch it to cover the escarole leaves. Align the edges of the dough and press, pinch, and wrap them over one another to create a well-sealed packet. Transfer to the prepared baking sheet and repeat with one more piece of dough.

Line a plate with paper towels and place it near the stove. Place a large nonstick skillet over medium-high heat and add 2 Tbsp of olive oil. Once shimmering, add the two prepared pies. Cook, checking the bottom of the dough occasionally and turning as needed, until crispy and well browned on both sides, 4 to 6 minutes per side. Transfer to the prepared plate.

While the pies are frying, create two more pies using some of the remaining balls of dough, escarole, and anchovies. Repeat the process, adding more olive oil to the pan as needed, until all the pies have been fried. Serve immediately.

The triumphant return of plump fava beans, waxy pea pods, pink radishes, and juicy strawberries is a perfect excuse to let the dominance of charcuterie and cheese fall away from the antipasti table and beckon fruits and vegetables, once again, to be the focus. In my dream world, I am friends with all the farmers at the greenmarkets and visit one every day with a pretty basket in tow and unlimited dollars to spend on treats. In reality, I get there as often as I can, narrowing in on a few special finds—like purple chive blossoms, which taste great sprinkled atop frittatas, or wispy, coiled garlic scapes, chopped and tucked inside breads before baking—and I use them to dress up the other, simpler foods I can always find easily at the grocery store. Whatever you come home with in your basket, spring is an abundant, happy time to be around the table, and motivation to throw open the windows, invite friends over, and prepare far too many beautiful dishes.

SPRING

BROCCOLINI FRITTATA

with torn, oil-packed anchovies or grated cheese

The master of frittatas who taught me everything I know, my Grandma Stella, would make a simple version of one every few days. She'd let the vegetables roll down from her fingers into a little pool of olive oil in the pan, cook them until tender, then add eggs and sometimes a sprinkling of grated Pecorino Romano. Unlike the American brunch versions of frittata, which are stacked high like deep-dish pies, Grandma's were thin, rarely using more than a handful of eggs and relying on flipping the frittata in the pan rather than roasting or broiling it.

In this variation, which you can finish in the oven for ease, I add a touch of thinly sliced garlic and black pepper for a little more depth. When it's done and cooled slightly, I sometimes drape the top with torn, oil-packed anchovies. It's meant to be a delicate dish, barely thicker than the broccolini.

6 large eggs

Kosher salt

Freshly ground black pepper

1 large [about 9-oz, or 255-g] bunch broccolini, or *broccolette*, ends trimmed, thick pieces halved lengthwise

1 Tbsp plus 2 tsp extra-virgin olive oil, plus more for drizzling, if desired

1 medium garlic clove, thinly sliced

Anchovies in oil, or a sprinkling of grated Pecorino Romano, Parmigiano-Reggiano, or feta cheese, for topping (optional)

SERVES 6 TO 8

If baking the frittata, preheat the oven to 400°F [200°C].

Meanwhile, set a medium pot of water—large enough to fit all the broccolini—over high heat to boil.

In a medium bowl, beat the eggs well. Season with about ⅛ tsp of salt and a generous pinch of pepper and set aside.

Set a large strainer in the sink. Once the pot of water is boiling rapidly, season it generously with salt and add the broccolini. Cook until the color is bright green and the stalks are slightly tenderized but still have good crunch, about 2½ minutes. Immediately strain and run under cold water until cool.

In a large [12-in, or 30.5-cm] nonstick ovenproof skillet over medium-high heat, combine the olive oil and garlic. Heat until the garlic just begins sizzling, about 1 minute. Lower the heat to medium-low and add the broccolini and a generous pinch each of salt and pepper. Cook, tossing the vegetables once or twice, until lightly coated in the oil, about 30 seconds.

Beat the eggs once more and pour them into the pan around and between the broccolini, tilting the pan and moving the eggs with a flexible spatula to fill the pan evenly. Lower the heat to medium and cook for 1 minute, all the while creating small holes in the bottom of the frittata with the spatula so more of the egg hits the bottom of the pan.

continued

If finishing the frittata in the oven, bake until the eggs are just set and slightly puffed at the top and not too browned underneath, 10 to 12 minutes. Alternatively, to cook the frittata completely on the stovetop, let the frittata continue cooking in the skillet until mostly set. Slide the partially cooked frittata onto a large flat plate. Place the empty, overturned skillet on top. Overturn the plate and pan in one swift motion to release the frittata back into the pan. Continue cooking on the second side until just cooked through in the center, 1 to 2 minutes more.

Remove the pan from the oven or stovetop and immediately use the spatula to loosen the frittata from the pan and slide it onto a large serving plate. (This prevents the bottom from overbrowning and the frittata from shrinking.) Sprinkle with more salt and pepper to taste—remember, the anchovies will be salty (if using).

Serve warm or at room temperature, topped with coarsely torn or chopped anchovies or drizzled very lightly with olive oil and sprinkled with cheese, as desired.

WARM OR CHILLED ARTICHOKES

with garlic-orange aioli

Artichokes are the gastronomic symbol of Rome and the regions surrounding it. In my family, artichokes also have the feeling of a celebratory food. This is largely because of their expense and the time commitment involved when making them—and because they're delicious and beloved and look special when arranged on a platter. On holidays, we stuff them with bread crumbs and garlic, then slow-steam them until tender.

This is a slightly speedier way to get your artichoke fix, and a more party-friendly way to serve them. You can eat them just after steaming, dipping each meaty leaf in some garlic-spiked aioli, or refrigerate them for up to a couple of days and serve chilled.

ARTICHOKES

1 large lemon, halved

3 large artichokes [about 2 lb, or 910 g, total]

Kosher salt

Extra-virgin olive oil, for rubbing the artichokes (optional)

AIOLI

¼ cup [60 g] mayonnaise

1 Tbsp plus 1 tsp extra-virgin olive oil

2 tsp fresh orange juice

¼ tsp finely grated orange zest

1½ tsp finely grated fresh garlic

Generous pinch of kosher salt

Pinch of freshly ground black pepper

SERVES 6

PREPARE THE ARTICHOKES: Fill a large bowl halfway with cool water and squeeze the juice of the lemon into the bowl. Add the squeezed lemon halves to the bowl, too.

Using scissors, snip off the tips of each artichoke leaf. Peel away the outermost part of the long stems using a vegetable peeler. Using a chef's knife, halve each artichoke lengthwise from tip to stem. Use a spoon to remove the hairy chokes and the fibrous innermost leaves from the center of each half and discard. Transfer the cleaned artichoke halves to the lemon water and repeat.

In a medium-large pot, pour the lemon water to reach about 1 in [2.5 cm] up the sides. Add the artichoke halves and cover the pot. Bring the liquid to a strong simmer over medium heat and cook, rotating the positions of the artichokes occasionally with tongs, until the hearts are tender when poked with a paring knife and the leaves remove somewhat easily when tugged, 35 to 40 minutes. Check the water level occasionally, adding more if the pan nears dry.

MEANWHILE, MAKE THE AIOLI: In a small bowl, combine all ingredients and stir well. Taste and adjust the seasonings as needed.

Transfer the artichokes to a serving bowl or platter. Sprinkle generously on all sides with kosher salt. If you're serving the artichokes immediately, you can rub them lightly with some olive oil, too. Serve warm, at room temperature, or chilled, encouraging guests to pluck the leaves and dip them into the aioli before eating the tender parts and the hearts.

RAINBOW CHARD
AND BLACK-EYED PEAS

with radishes

In Italy, cooked black-eyed peas are often served as a side dish to accompany boiled or roasted meats. One of my grandfathers, whose parents hailed from Calabria, taught us to stew them with softened onion and Swiss chard, the quick-cooking spring green. In this variation on a dish that's less brothy than his, I use rainbow chard for a burst of color, and drizzle the dish in flavorful olive oil to finish. Though Grandpa never would have used them, some lightly cooked radishes also add something to crunch on.

3 Tbsp extra-virgin olive oil, plus more for drizzling

½ medium yellow onion, thinly sliced

Kosher salt

Freshly ground black pepper

2 large garlic cloves, finely chopped

1¾ cups [298 g] drained black-eyed peas [from one 15-oz, or 430-g, can]

3 cups [108 g] coarsely torn rainbow chard or Swiss chard leaves, from about 1 bunch, large stems and very thick spines removed, small stems finely chopped

4 oz [115 g] quartered French breakfast radishes or similar

Flaky sea salt, for garnishing

SERVES 4 TO 6

In a large pot over medium heat, heat the olive oil. Add the onion, a pinch of kosher salt, and a few pinches of pepper. Cook, stirring occasionally, until the onion is well softened, about 3 minutes. Stir in the garlic and cook for 30 seconds more. Add the black-eyed peas and ¾ cup [180 ml] of fresh water. Cook, stirring occasionally, until warmed through, about 2 minutes. Add the chard leaves and radishes and cook, stirring constantly, until the chard just wilts, 1 to 2 minutes. Taste and adjust the seasoning as needed.

Transfer the mixture to a large shallow serving bowl or rimmed platter. Drizzle lightly with olive oil, sprinkle with sea salt and a little more pepper, and serve warm or at room temperature.

SHAVED FENNEL SALAD

with sweet peas and avocado

While you can't let salad greens sit out for long, a fresh chilled fennel bulb retains its crunch over time, perfect for gatherings. When sliced very thinly and seasoned with citrusy vinaigrette, it keeps just a delicate hint of its anise flavor. I like to pair and balance it with a few things fatty and sweet—in this case, ripe avocado, spring peas, nutty cheese, and dried fruit. This salad is endlessly adaptable: sprinkle it with any toasted dried nut or seed, use basil instead of parsley, or play with combinations of different fruits, cheeses, or citrus juices in the vinaigrette.

2 fennel bulbs [3 cups, or 255 g], thinly sliced on a mandoline

¼ loosely packed cup [1 g] torn fennel fronds

3½ oz [100 g] sugar snap peas, sliced on the diagonal

½ small red onion, very thinly sliced on a mandoline

¼ cup [10 g] coarsely chopped fresh flat-leaf parsley

3 Tbsp fresh lemon juice

2 Tbsp plus 1 tsp extra-virgin olive oil

1 Tbsp fresh lime juice

Salt

Freshly ground black pepper

½ firm-ripe avocado, thinly sliced

Pecorino Romano or Parmigiano-Reggiano cheese, shaved into thin ribbons with a vegetable peeler, for garnishing

2 tsp dried currants or finely chopped toasted hazelnuts

SERVES 4

In a serving bowl, combine the fennel slices and fronds, snap peas, red onion, parsley, lemon juice, olive oil, lime juice, and a pinch each of salt and pepper. Toss to combine. Add the avocado slices and toss gently to incorporate.

Top the salad with about 12 slices of thinly shaved cheese, sprinkle with the currants, and serve.

SALMON RILLETTES

with cornichon, shallots, and mustard

The Italians don't really do rillettes like the French, but they do serve fish preserved in fat—like oil-packed tuna or tuna belly (*ventresca di tonno*)—as part of an antipasti or salad course. I love this pickle-y, bright-colored salmon spread for serving with good sea salt crackers or olive oil crostini. It's best prepared and refrigerated for a few hours, or even a day, ahead, but you can serve or eat it just-cooled if guests are on their way. If you're one of those people who doesn't like pickled cucumbers, use the equivalent of finely diced celery or capers instead of the cornichons.

2 small shallots, one halved lengthwise, one finely chopped [1 Tbsp plus 1 tsp]

¾ cup [180 ml] dry white wine

2 tsp red wine vinegar

½ tsp kosher salt

¼ tsp freshly ground black pepper

1 lb [455 g] fresh wild coho or Alaskan salmon fillet (or frozen is fine), skin and bones removed, if possible

¼ cup [60 g] mayonnaise

1 Tbsp plus 2 tsp grainy Dijon mustard

¼ cup [about 10 small cornichons, or 35 g] thinly sliced cornichons

2 Tbsp cornichon juice, from the jar

Finely chopped fresh tarragon, dill, or chives, for garnishing (optional)

Good crackers, such as Olive Oil and Sea Salt Crackers with Whole Wheat (page 38) or Grilled Crostini (page 39), for serving

MAKES 1 PINT [ABOUT 575 G]; SERVES 8

See photo page 96

In a medium, high-sided skillet over medium-high heat, combine the halved shallot, white wine, ½ cup water, 1 tsp of vinegar, ⅛ tsp of pepper, and ¼ tsp of kosher salt. Bring to a low boil. Add the salmon. Cook, turning occasionally, until just cooked through and no longer slimy in the center, about 3 minutes per side for fresh salmon or 8 minutes per side for frozen.

Remove the fish from the liquid and transfer to a plate. Peel away any skin, bones, or gray pieces of flesh and discard. Sprinkle the meat with ⅛ tsp of salt and refrigerate until cool, 10 to 15 minutes.

Meanwhile, in a medium bowl, stir together the mayonnaise, mustard, cornichons and juice, and the remaining 1 tsp of red wine vinegar.

Break the salmon into bite-size pieces and add to the bowl with the mayonnaise mixture. Season with the remaining ⅛ tsp each of salt and pepper and stir gently to combine. Taste and adjust the seasonings as needed.

You can serve immediately or, ideally, cover the bowl or transfer the rillettes to a jar and refrigerate for a few hours, or up to 1 day. Sprinkle with the herbs, if desired, and serve with crackers.

Readying Rillettes

The best vessels for storing and serving these salmon rillettes are wide-mouth jars, such as those made by Weck, which allow you to scoop them up easily with a small spoon, fork, or spreading tool such as a cheese knife. If you don't have the right size jar, rillettes work perfectly well served in any bowl you might use for dip, with the crackers or crostini strewn around it.

FARRO SALAD

with raw and seared mushrooms and celery

Having a few types of grains always on hand means you can whip up a dish with little more than the odds and ends in your refrigerator or pantry. Farro, a chewy, oblong type grown in the rugged mountainous regions of northern Italy, is one I often save for visitors, because it feels more special and elegant than rice or pasta. Deeply seared mushrooms give this dish a satisfying flavor, while delicate, thinly sliced raw mushrooms give it a light crunch and fanciness.

1¼ cups [225 g] uncooked farro

1¼ tsp kosher salt, plus more as needed

5 Tbsp [75 ml] extra-virgin olive oil

6 oz [170 g] cremini (baby bella) or white button mushrooms, about 12 medium mushrooms, sliced

1 large garlic clove, minced

1 large [60-g] celery stalk, halved lengthwise and thinly sliced

¼ cup [60 ml] distilled white vinegar

¼ packed cup [10 g] coarsely chopped fresh Italian parsley leaves

Freshly ground black pepper

SERVES 6

A Dish That Lasts

Though you'll lose the pretty whiteness of the raw mushrooms if you make this dish ahead, the rest of the ingredients keep their wonderful chew and texture into the next day, when the dish is just as—or maybe even more—delicious.

In a medium saucepan, combine the farro, 6 cups [1.4 L] of water, and 1 tsp of salt. Bring to a boil over high heat, then lower the heat to a simmer. Cook until the farro is just tender (it will still be a bit chewy), 15 to 17 minutes. Strain and transfer to a serving bowl.

Meanwhile, in a large skillet over medium-high heat, heat 1 Tbsp of olive oil until shimmering. Add half the sliced mushrooms (the oil should sizzle when you add them) and season with ⅛ tsp of salt. Cook, barely stirring so the mushrooms get well seared, until lightly browned all over and cooked through, about 4 minutes.

Transfer the mushrooms into the bowl with the farro. Lower the heat under the pan to medium and add the remaining 4 Tbsp [60 ml] of olive oil, the garlic, and ⅛ tsp of salt. Cook, stirring, until the garlic is lightly golden in places, 1 minute.

Transfer the oil and garlic to the bowl with the farro and mushrooms. Add the celery and vinegar and stir to combine. Let rest a few minutes to cool slightly.

Stir in the remaining half of the sliced mushrooms and the parsley. Taste and season with salt and pepper as needed. Serve slightly warm or at room temperature, or refrigerate overnight and serve lightly chilled.

WHITE WINE CLAMS

with barley, kale, and fennel seed

My siblings' and my clam addiction started early, while we were growing up with bowls of linguini and white clam sauce as part of our Italian seven fishes dinner every Christmas Eve, and buckets of steamers consumed on every East Coast summer vacation. One of the best ways to eat clams is in a pool of their own naturally salty juices, which make up the base of this succulent, brothy barley dish enhanced with a little fennel seed, tangy mustard, and kale.

2 lb [910 g] cockles or other small clams, scrubbed and rinsed under cool water

1 cup [200 g] uncooked barley

2 tsp kosher salt

2 Tbsp extra-virgin olive oil

3 large garlic cloves, thinly sliced

¼ tsp whole fennel seeds

⅓ cup [80 ml] white wine

½ tsp Dijon mustard

1 packed cup [15 g] chopped Tuscan (dino or lacinato) kale leaves

SERVES 6

See photo page 102

Purge the cockles to remove residual sand (see Sidebar, page 103). Drain.

Fill a medium pot two-thirds of the way with water and bring to a boil over high heat. Add the barley and salt. Cook until tender, about 30 minutes. Strain well and set aside in either a wide shallow serving bowl or deep-rimmed platter.

Set the remaining ingredients and ⅓ cup [80 ml] of fresh water individually next to the stove. In a medium pot over medium-high heat, combine the olive oil, garlic, and fennel seeds. Cook, stirring, until the oil is simmering and the garlic is fragrant but not yet browned, about 2 minutes. Add the water, wine, and mustard and stir to incorporate. Raise the heat to high and bring the liquid to a strong simmer. Add the clams and cover the pot. Cook until they just begin to open, 3 minutes. Add the kale and cover the pot again. Cook until the kale wilts and all the clams have fully opened, 1 to 2 minutes more. Discard any clams that do not open.

Using a slotted spoon, transfer the clams and kale to a medium bowl. Pour or spoon most of the juices atop the barley, leaving behind in the pot the last few Tbsp, which may contain some sand or impurities. (You can discard this.) Spread the barley into a thin layer. Top with the clams and kale and serve immediately.

How to Purge Clams

Fill a large bowl halfway with cold water and stir
in 1 tsp of kosher salt. Add the clams (they should
be fully submerged) and transfer to the refrigerator for at least 15 minutes and up to 40. Using a
slotted spoon or your hands, transfer the clams to
a strainer, leaving the sand behind in the bowl, and
rinse thoroughly with cool water.

GRILLED BACON-WRAPPED LEEKS

with honey glaze

Northern Italians know their way around a leek (*porro*). In the upper regions of the country, the best recipes often feature them oven-braised with decadent delights like melted butter, eggs, and Parmigiano-Reggiano. They can also be sautéed in lardo or pork fat, so, keeping with that theme, I roll mine inside a thick strip of bacon before sending them to the grill—my favorite place to cook them since they take on a lovely smoky note and crispy edges. Start them over indirect heat to render some of the bacon fat and tenderize the vegetable fibers, then finish over high heat to crisp the meat and edges. Add a pinch of cayenne pepper to the honey glaze if you like a hint of spice.

4 slender leeks [each about 1 in, or 2.5 cm, thick], halved lengthwise, roots left intact

1 Tbsp honey

1 Tbsp fresh lemon juice

⅛ tsp kosher salt

Freshly ground black pepper

8 smoked bacon slices [8 oz, or 230 g]

SERVES 8

Trim the green ends of the leeks of any especially tough or dark sections—the leeks should be no longer than 10 in [25 cm] after trimming. Rinse them thoroughly under cold running water, rubbing and separating the layers with your fingers as needed to remove any grit. Pat dry.

In a medium bowl, whisk the honey, lemon juice, salt, a pinch of pepper, and 1 Tbsp of water until the honey dissolves. Brush the cut sides of the leeks generously with the honey mixture, then carefully wrap each with 1 bacon slice, starting about 1 in [2.5 cm] up from the bottom of the leek stems and overlapping the bacon slightly (try starting and ending the bacon wrapping on the cut side of the leeks).

Preheat a grill to medium heat. If using a charcoal grill, arrange the coals in the center, leaving about 3 in [7.5 cm] for indirect heat cooking around the edges of the grill.

Transfer the leeks to the hot grate on their backs, positioning them around the edges of the grill if working with charcoal. Cover the grill and cook, turning once, until the bacon is browned and cooked through, and the leeks are tender, about 16 minutes total. Transfer the leeks to the center of the grill (slightly more direct heat) for 2 to 3 more minutes of direct-heat cooking to complete crisping the bacon and char the edges of the leeks. Transfer to a platter and serve.

MINI PROSCIUTTO AND PECORINO PANINI

on strawberry buttermilk biscuits

Most sandwiches in Italy are delightfully simple, containing little more than a few slices of cured meat and cheese between a roll. I swapped the bread for fluffy, crispy-edged biscuits with ripe, in-season strawberries. These mini prosciutto and cheese sandwiches work both as an antipasto or small meal.

One trick to making great biscuits is to work quickly and confidently, keeping every ingredient as cold as possible. Use frozen butter. Stay speedy. And don't worry about perfection. Even an oddly shaped biscuit can be delicious.

1 cup [2 sticks, or 226 g] unsalted butter, frozen solid

3 Tbsp unsalted butter (not frozen), for melting and brushing

3 cups [390 g] unbleached all-purpose flour, plus more for dusting

2 tsp baking powder

2 tsp sugar

¾ tsp kosher salt

½ tsp baking soda

⅛ tsp finely grated lemon zest (optional)

Pinch of freshly ground black pepper

1¼ cups [300 ml] buttermilk, shaken before using

1 heaping cup [5 oz, or 140 g] thinly sliced fresh strawberries

At least 18 thin slices prosciutto

At least 18 very thin slices Pecorino Romano cheese

MAKES 18 PETITE SANDWICHES

Working quickly, grate the frozen butter on the large side of a box grater and place the shavings in a bowl. Immediately transfer them back to the freezer.

In a large bowl, combine the flour, baking powder, sugar, salt, baking soda, lemon zest (if using), and pepper. Add the grated butter and stir with your fingers to combine. Place the bowl in the freezer for at least 10 minutes and up to 30.

Retrieve the bowl. Line a large baking sheet with parchment paper and transfer it to the freezer. Pour the buttermilk into the flour mixture, stirring with a fork a few times to incorporate. Add the strawberries and begin gently kneading the dough with your hands just until it comes together.

Working quickly, lightly flour a work surface and place the dough on top of it. Dust the top of the dough with flour and lightly flour a rolling pin. Roll the dough into a 6-by-12-in [15-by-30.5-cm] rectangle (page 108), pressing in the edges as needed to keep the dough in one solid mass. Fold the short ends of the dough toward each other, folding the dough into thirds like a letter and piling the dough on top of itself. Alternatively, slice the dough crosswise into three equal pieces and place the pieces on top of each other. Roll the dough again into a 6-by-12-in [15-by-30.5-cm] rectangle, sprinkling lightly with more flour as needed to prevent sticking.

continued

Repeat the folding and rolling three more times. You should end with the dough rolled out to a 6-by-12-in [15-by-30.5-cm] rectangle, a little more than 1 in [2.5 cm] thick.

Remove the baking sheet from the freezer. Working quickly and using a very sharp, lightly floured knife, cut the dough lengthwise and crosswise about every 2 in [5 cm] to divide it into about eighteen 2-in [5-cm] squares. Alternatively, for larger biscuits, slice the dough into 12 equal, slightly larger rectangles. Arrange the biscuits, separated slightly, on the baking sheet and transfer the sheet to the freezer for 15 minutes.

Preheat the oven to 450°F [230°C] and set a rack in the top third of the oven.

Meanwhile, melt the remaining 3 Tbsp of butter.

When the oven is preheated, remove the biscuits from the freezer and brush the tops with the melted butter. Bake without opening the door until the biscuits have risen and turned golden brown on the top, about 24 minutes. While they bake, butter will melt out onto the bottom of the pan, but will eventually evaporate toward the end of baking.

Remove the baking sheet and transfer the biscuits to a rack to let cool ever so slightly. Split each like a sandwich, layer with one or two pieces of prosciutto and a few shavings of Pecorino Romano, and serve.

ROASTED RADISHES AND THEIR GREENS

with sliced ricotta salata, walnuts, and olive oil

Roasting a radish with its greens still attached makes you realize how delicious and beautiful unelaborate food can be. In Italy, you're more likely to see a turnip used than a radish for roasting—in fact, you can use this same preparation with baby turnips, just add about 10 minutes to the roasting time. But I love the magenta skins of cooked radishes and how much the spicy vegetable mellows as it cooks.

Ricotta salata is a pure white, crumbly, rindless cheese that originated in Sicily. You can use it grated or crumbled like you would feta, but it's not nearly as tangy. Here, I like it sprinkled generously in thin shavings (I use a vegetable peeler) atop the finished vegetables.

2 large bunches [1½ lb, or 680 g, total] round red radishes with leaves attached, radishes halved through the stems, very large leaves trimmed

3 Tbsp extra-virgin olive oil, plus more for serving

⅛ tsp kosher salt

Freshly ground black pepper

2 Tbsp very thinly sliced ricotta salata cheese or good-quality feta cheese

2 Tbsp very finely chopped or smashed walnuts, pistachios, or hazelnuts

SERVES 6 TO 8

Preheat the oven to 350°F [180°C].

On a large baking sheet lined with aluminum foil, if desired, spread the radishes and their leaves in a single layer. Drizzle with the olive oil and season generously with the salt and some pepper, tossing and rubbing to coat.

Roast until the radishes are crisp-tender and the greens are frizzled, about 10 minutes.

Transfer the radishes to a large serving platter. Scatter the cheese and walnuts atop the radishes, drizzle lightly with more olive oil and sprinkle with pepper, and serve.

BABY ROOT VEGETABLES

in coriander vinaigrette

This petite vegetable medley, flecked with coriander seeds and flaky sea salt, makes a perky little antipasto on its own or a vegetable accompaniment to a cheese plate, charcuterie board, or dip plate. The al dente vegetables can also be a colorful topping for ricotta tartlets (opposite page) or a pizza bianco. You can cook these vegetables hours ahead and store them at room temperature. If they've been sitting, stir them to coat in the spiced vinaigrette a final time just before serving.

1 to 1¼ lb [455 to 570 g] small trimmed baby root vegetables, such as golden beets, radishes, Thumbelina or very small carrots, and turnips

Carrot tops or fresh cilantro or parsley leaves, for garnishing

4 Tbsp [2 oz, or 56 g] unsalted butter

2 tsp whole coriander seeds, coarsely ground, chopped, or smashed

½ tsp caraway seeds

½ tsp kosher salt

2 large lemons

2 Tbsp extra-virgin olive oil

Flaky sea salt, for garnishing (optional)

SERVES 4, OR MAKES ENOUGH
FOR 1 BATCH BABY ROOT VEGETABLE
AND RICOTTA TARTLETS (OPPOSITE PAGE)

Peel and discard any exceptionally thick skins from the vegetables (such as on the beets), and trim the ends of the remaining vegetables as needed, leaving maybe a little bit of the greens atop the carrots, beets, and turnips for prettiness. Reserve any carrot tops for garnish. Cut any larger vegetables in half or slice them lengthwise (no piece should be much thicker than about ½ in, or 12 mm).

In a medium, heavy-bottomed pot over medium heat, combine the butter, ¼ cup [60 ml] of water, and half each of the coriander and caraway seeds and kosher salt. Cook until the butter melts. Add the radishes and turnips and cook just until lightly tenderized, 1 to 1½ minutes. Remove using a slotted spoon and transfer to a medium serving bowl.

To the pot, add the golden beets and carrots and cook, stirring occasionally, until the carrots are slightly tender but still have a bite, 6 to 8 minutes. At this point the butter will have started to brown and caramelize; if it gets too dark or syrupy, add 1 Tbsp more water as needed. Fish out the carrots and transfer to the bowl while you cook the beets until tender, 4 to 6 minutes longer. Transfer the beets to the bowl. Discard the butter mixture.

In the bowl with the vegetables, add the juice of 2 lemons, the olive oil, the remaining coriander and caraway seeds and kosher salt, and 2 to 3 Tbsp of the reserved torn carrot tops or herb leaves. Toss to coat. Sprinkle with sea salt, if desired, and serve immediately or let rest at room temperature for up to a few hours before serving.

BABY ROOT VEGETABLE AND RICOTTA TARTLETS

on salt and pepper pastry dough

Because the flaky dough stays crisp and sturdy both when warm and at room temperature, these tartlets remain delicious long after they have cooled.

DOUGH

2 cups [260 g] unbleached all-purpose flour, plus more for dusting

½ tsp kosher salt

¼ tsp freshly ground black pepper

6 oz [1½ sticks, or 170 g] cold unsalted butter, chopped into ½-in [12-mm] cubes

½ cup [120 ml] ice-cold water

Extra-virgin olive oil, for brushing

Flaky sea salt, for garnishing

RICOTTA TOPPING

16 oz [455 g] whole-milk ricotta

2 Tbsp extra-virgin olive oil, plus more as needed

½ tsp kosher salt

⅛ tsp finely grated lemon zest

BABY ROOT VEGETABLE TOPPING

1 batch Baby Root Vegetables in Coriander Vinaigrette (previous page)

MAKES 12 TO 15 TARTLETS

MAKE THE DOUGH AT LEAST 1 HOUR, AND UP TO 1 DAY, BEFORE YOU PLAN TO BAKE THE TARTLETS: In a large food processor (or a large bowl), add the flour, salt, and pepper and mix briefly. Add the butter pieces and either pulse about ten times in the food processor or work the pieces into the flour by hand or using a pastry cutter until only pea-size crumbs remain. Slowly trickle in the cold water, pulsing or stirring to incorporate. The dough should feel moist with little pebbles of visible butter and hold together when pinched.

Turn out onto a large piece of plastic wrap and use the ends of the wrap and pressure from your hands to form it into a ball. Cover the dough completely with the wrap and press down on the top and sides to form into a 1-in-[2.5-cm-] thick square. Refrigerate for at least 1 hour, or up to overnight.

MEANWHILE, PREPARE THE TOPPINGS: Clean out the food processor and add the ricotta, olive oil, salt, and lemon zest. Process until silky but not at all runny (as ricotta consistency can vary, if needed for smoothness, add 1 Tbsp more olive oil). Cover and refrigerate until ready to use.

Prepare the Baby Root Vegetables in Coriander Vinaigrette.

continued

Preheat the oven to 400°F [200°C] and set a rack in the top third of the oven. Line a baking sheet with parchment paper.

Unwrap the dough and transfer it to a lightly floured work surface. Using a rolling pin, roll the dough ¼ in [6 mm] thick, frequently rotating it and adding more flour underneath and on top as needed to prevent sticking (you will have about a 14-in [35.5-cm] square; it does not need to be perfect). Working quickly using biscuit or cookie cutters or a sharp knife, cut into tartlet shapes, such as 2- to 3-in [5- to 7.5-cm] circles or 1-by-3-in [2.5-by-7.5-cm] rectangles. Transfer them to the lined baking sheet. Place the baking sheet in the refrigerator for 10 minutes.

Working quickly, spread a generous amount of the ricotta mixture onto each tartlet, leaving a ¼- to ½-in [6- to 12-mm] border on all sides. Lightly brush the exposed edges with olive oil. Top each tartlet with an array of vegetables (reserve the sauce from the vegetables in the bowl for later), nearly covering the ricotta—add more than you think, as the vegetables shrink during baking.

Bake until the pastry looks puffy and lightly browned on the edges, about 35 minutes. Remove and drizzle the tartlets lightly with the reserved sauce from the vegetables. Garnish with small pieces of the carrot tops (reserved while preparing the vegetables) and sprinkle with sea salt. Serve hot or at room temperature.

WHITE CLAM PIZZAS

with scallion and bacon

Served in small shapes or slices and with light, bright toppings, little pizzas, or *pizzette*, make the best antipasti. In particular, watching this juicy, garlicky clam pie win over guests never gets old for me. It's my riff on the white clam pies I ate at Connecticut pizzerias growing up, and nixes the classic cheese topping for a thin, silky sauce of cream and fresh clam juice that's baked right on top—the kind of briny, satisfying concoction you can't fully grasp until you try it. Have a generous hand with the parsley, scallions, bacon, and chili flakes, which—in addition to the sauce and fresh, juicy clams—make this pie vibrant, addictive, and memorable.

3 lb [1.4 kg] cockles, about 5 dozen, or other small clams, shells rinsed under cold water

4 bacon slices [4 oz or 115 g], cooked and chopped

One 8-fl-oz [240-ml] bottle clam juice, or substitute water

⅔ cup [160 ml] heavy cream

2 large garlic cloves, finely chopped

Kosher salt

Freshly ground black pepper

All-purpose flour, for dusting

Two 8-oz [230-g] pizza dough balls, store-bought or from your favorite pizza place, fully risen and at room temperature

Extra-virgin olive oil, for brushing

½ cup [70 g] thinly sliced scallion, light green and white parts, from about 7 scallions

Grated Parmigiano-Reggiano, for garnishing (optional)

Chopped fresh Italian parsley, for garnishing

Chili flakes, for serving (optional)

MAKES TWO 11-IN [28-CM] PIZZAS

Purge the clams (see Sidebar, page 103) and cook the bacon before starting.

Preheat the oven to 525°F [275°C] and set a pizza stone, a rimless metal baking sheet, or an overturned sturdy metal baking sheet in the top third of the oven (make sure it's level).

Set a medium heat-proof bowl next to the stove. In a medium pot over high heat, heat the clam juice or water until boiling. Add the clams and cover the pot. Cook until a few of the clams have begun to open, 1 to 2 minutes. Remove the lid and continue cooking until most of the clams begin opening, 2 to 3 minutes more. As they open, transfer the clams to the bowl using a slotted spoon. When the clams have all opened, turn off the heat (discard any clams that do not open). Reserve the juices in the pot. Pick the meat from the shells and coarsely chop.

Skim ⅓ cup [80 ml] of clam juices from the top of the pot, leaving behind any sand or impurities in the bottom. Discard the remaining clam juice and clean out the pot. Add the reserved juice back to the pot as well as the cream, garlic, a pinch of salt, and a generous pinch of pepper. Bring to a simmer over medium heat. Cook, watching carefully, until thickened slightly, about 3 minutes. Remove from the heat.

Lightly flour a large piece of parchment paper and set it atop a large, flat cutting board, or generously flour a pizza peel.

continued

Working one at a time, stretch a ball of pizza dough into a 10- to 11-in [25- to 28-cm] diameter round (go as thinly as you can without breaking the dough or making it too weak). Place it on the prepared parchment or pizza peel.

Working quickly, brush the top of the dough generously with olive oil and season lightly with salt and pepper. Leaving a ½-in [12-mm] border around the edges, drizzle the dough with half of the cream mixture [about ½ cup, or 120 ml]. The pizza may look overly saucy, but will dry significantly as it cooks. Top with half each of the clams, scallions, and bacon, and a sprinkling of Parmigiano, if desired.

Carefully slide the parchment paper from the cutting board or the pizza from the peel onto the preheated pizza stone or pan. Bake until the dough is crisped and golden and the sauce has thickened, 10 to 12 minutes if using a pizza stone, or 12 to 14 minutes if using a baking sheet. Remove and repeat with the remaining dough and toppings. Slice and serve the pizzas as they come out, sprinkled with fresh parsley leaves and chili flakes.

CASTELVETRANO OLIVE SALAD

with garlic and celery

This green olive and celery salad, inspired by the traditional versions from southern Italy, is meaty, juicy, and garlicky. Castelvetrano olives, which are from Sicily but can be found in most grocery stores, have a crisp-tender texture and sweet, buttery flavor.

Though it would seem easier to buy pitted olives, don't fall victim to this shortcut. The texture and flavor do not compare to pitting them yourselves, an inexplicable mystery that's worth the smashing and peeling every time.

1¼ lb [570 g] Castelvetrano olives with pits [about 6 cups]

8 to 10 inner celery stalks with their leaves [14 oz, or 400 g, total], sliced ¼ in [6 mm] thick on a diagonal [about 4 cups]

¼ cup [60 ml] extra-virgin olive oil

2 Tbsp red wine vinegar

2 medium garlic cloves, finely chopped

Scant ¼ tsp kosher salt

⅛ tsp freshly ground black pepper

SERVES 6 TO 8

See photo page 119

To pit the olives, lay them, one by one, on a stable cutting board and smash them semi-firmly with the broad side of a chef's knife. Remove the flesh in large pieces, such as halves, and discard the pits. You should have about 3½ cups pitted olive pieces when done.

In a large serving bowl, combine the olives, sliced celery, olive oil, vinegar, and garlic. Sprinkle with the salt and pepper and stir well to coat. Let rest at least 15 minutes and up to a few hours at room temperature. Toss again before serving.

MIXED FISH CRUDO

with olive oil, dill, and chives

Crudo means "raw" in Italian, and on a menu the word can refer to any seafood served chilled and raw. In southern coastal Italy, for example, platters of mixed crudo including shrimp, clams, mussels, calamari, and more are commonly shared as antipasti. In America, we've largely come to know crudo as delicate slices of raw fish fillet, often served with subtle garnishes. Incredibly fresh fish is key here—be sure it smells neutral and not strong or fishy, and that the color looks untainted. The fish listed here are suggestions, but go with whatever wild fish your fishmonger knows is fresh that day, tastes good raw, and will slice easily without becoming mushy.

1 lb [455 g] highest-quality chilled raw fish steaks, preferably a mix of tuna loin, fluke, and/or hamachi (you can also use black bass, rockfish, or wild salmon)

3 Tbsp extra-virgin olive oil, for drizzling

Juice from ¼ lemon, or to taste

2 loosely packed Tbsp fresh dill flowers, or 1 Tbsp finely chopped fresh dill

2 tsp minced fresh chives

Heaping ¼ tsp flaky sea salt

Freshly ground black pepper

SERVES 4

Ask your fishmonger to slice the fish into very thin, broad pieces (they should be at least ⅛ in [4 mm] thin, but it doesn't really matter how wide), or do it yourself using a very sharp fillet knife or Santoku knife. (If needed, you can place the fish in the freezer for 10 minutes to firm it up before slicing, or run your knife under cold water between each slice.) Trim away any unsightly pieces. If desired, on a clean, stable work surface, place the fish between two pieces of parchment paper and very gently pound it even thinner with a firm, flat tool such as a meat pounder or the bottom of a heavy glass measuring cup.

Transfer the fish slices to a large flat platter, arranging the pieces in groups by color (they should touch but not overlap much). Drizzle evenly with the olive oil, then squeeze some lemon juice on top. Sprinkle with the dill flowers, chives, flaky sea salt, and pepper. Serve immediately.

CHILLED VEGETABLE PLATTER

with white bean dip and pistachio pesto

Come springtime when the market vegetable bins look like a painter's palette again, I can't resist grabbing anything and everything beautiful and creating a platter. In ancient Roman times, serving any cold dish or ice-soaked ingredient was considered a luxury. Bitter vegetables were and still are a favorite to eat chilled, often with simple dips or olive oil. Feel free to use this recipe as a blueprint or play with any vegetables or fruits you find.

Kosher salt

1 medium [6-oz, or 170-g] fennel bulb, trimmed and sliced lengthwise into thin wedges

Small or baby carrots [about 6 oz, or 170 g], greens left intact, if desired, scrubbed well

Cauliflower florets [about 6 oz, or 170 g], broken into bite-size pieces

Romanesco florets [about 6 oz, or 170 g], broken into bite-size pieces

Winter radishes [about 5 oz, or 140 g], such as black, scrubbed well and thinly sliced into rounds or cut into small wedges

Breakfast radishes [about 4 oz, or 115 g], small greens attached

Green beans or yellow beans [about 4 oz, or 115 g], trimmed

1 small [3-oz, or 85-g] Chioggia beet, peeled and very thinly sliced

Ripe baby strawberries or fresh red currants, for garnishing (optional)

White Bean Dip (page 122), for serving

Pistachio Pesto (page 123), for serving

SERVES 10 TO 12

Add the vegetables to one or more bowls and fill with cold water; add a few generous pinches of salt and stir gently to dissolve. Refrigerate unti ready to serve, at least 15 minutes and up to half a day.

When ready to serve, drain the vegetables and pat dry. Arrange the vegetables on a platter in a pleasing way and garnish with the strawberries, if desired. Place the warm or room-temperature bean dip and room-temperature pistachio pesto each in a small bowl and nestle them among the vegetables.

Serve immediately, while the vegetables are still chilled and the dips are fresh.

Crudités Secret

Soaking raw vegetables in cold salt water in the fridge is my favorite trick to keeping them perky and flavorful, and it also helps mellow the flavor of particularly spicy ones, like radishes. Scrub, rinse, and trim them first. In a large bowl or a few small bowls, combine the vegetables and enough cold water to cover. Season generously with a few pinches of salt and refrigerate until ready to use, at least 15 minutes and up to about 12 hours. Remove, drain well, and pat dry.

WHITE BEAN DIP

with bacon, rosemary, and peppercorns

This creamy dip clings well to raw vegetables and tastes great either warm or at room temperature.

1 bacon slice [about 1 oz, or 30 g], chopped or snipped with scissors into small pieces

One 15-oz [430-g] can cannellini beans, rinsed well and drained

1 garlic clove, minced

⅛ tsp kosher salt, plus more to taste

¼ tsp onion powder

6 Tbsp [90 ml] plus 1 tsp extra-virgin olive oil

2 Tbsp fresh lemon juice

Finely chopped fresh rosemary, for garnishing

Freshly ground pink or black peppercorns

Flaky sea salt (optional)

MAKES 1¼ CUPS [285 G]

See photo page 121

In a medium skillet over medium heat, cook the bacon pieces, stirring frequently, until crispy and deeply browned, 4 to 6 minutes. Transfer the bacon pieces to a small bowl and leave the fat in the pan.

To the hot pan with the fat, add the cannellini beans and garlic. Cook, stirring occasionally, until the beans look dry and the garlic smells aromatic, 1 to 2 minutes. Turn off the heat.

In the bowl of a food processor, combine the bean mixture, ⅛ tsp of salt, and the onion powder. With the motor running, stream in 6 Tbsp [90 ml] of olive oil and the lemon juice and process until almost smooth. Taste and adjust the seasoning as necessary.

You can serve this dip warm or at room temperature. Do the final step just before serving to prevent a film from forming on top: Transfer the dip to a small bowl and, using a spoon, create shallow swirls around the surface of the dip (like a bull's-eye). In the swirls, drizzle in the remaining 1 tsp of olive oil and sprinkle with the reserved bacon along with a little rosemary and pepper to taste. Sprinkle with sea salt (if using) and serve immediately.

PISTACHIO PESTO

Common in Sicily, pistachio pastes are either savory—like this pesto, flecked with garlic and herbs and loosened with plenty of olive oil—or served inside sweet pastries. Save any extra pesto for tossing into roasted or grilled vegetables or slathering on toasts or sandwiches.

1 cup [4¾ oz, or 135 g] raw shelled pistachios

¾ cup [180 ml] extra-virgin olive oil, or more as needed

1½ cups [18 g] fresh basil leaves

½ cup [6 g] fresh mint leaves

⅓ cup plus 2 Tbsp [30 g] freshly grated, loosely packed Pecorino Romano cheese (if substituting pre-grated cheese, start with 2 Tbsp, and add more only to taste)

Kosher salt

Pinch of freshly ground black pepper

MAKES ABOUT 1½ CUPS [350 G]

See photo page 121

In a food processor, add the pistachios and process until the nuts are finely ground. Add the basil, mint, cheese, olive oil, and a generous pinch each of salt and pepper. Process until saucy but not completely smooth, adding a little more oil if needed to thin the consistency. Taste and adjust the seasoning as needed.

CRISPY PROSCIUTTO

or salami chips

After just a few minutes in the oven or a skillet, salty charcuterie slices turn into chips you can serve on their own as snacks or crumble onto vegetable dishes. Cook at a moderate heat to allow the fat to render gradually.

4 oz [115 g] very thinly sliced cured prosciutto or salami, about 12 slices

MAKES ABOUT 12

See photo page 9

OVEN METHOD

Preheat the oven to 350°F [180°C].

Tear or cut the prosciutto slices in half so each piece is only about 3 in [7.5 cm] long. On a large rimmed baking sheet, arrange the slices without overlapping. Transfer to the oven and bake until some of the fat has rendered, the pieces feel firm, and the edges are lightly browned, about 12 minutes. Remove, let cool slightly, and transfer to a paper towel–lined plate to drain slightly. The pieces will feel crisper as they cool. Serve or use warm or at room temperature.

SKILLET METHOD

Tear or cut the prosciutto slices in half so each piece is no more than 3 in [7.5 cm] long. In a large nonstick skillet, place as many slices as can fit without overlapping. Cook over medium heat until some of the fat has rendered and the pieces feel firm, 4 to 6 minutes. Transfer to a paper towel–lined plate to drain slightly. The pieces will feel crisper as they cool. Serve or use warm or at room temperature.

NANNY'S VEAL BRACIOLINI

I was a bit hesitant to share this recipe—it's that good, and that special to our family. It was passed down to us from one of our Italian great-grandmothers, who we called Nanny, and eventually taught to us by our 100-year-old Great-Uncle Joe. Everyone who tasted these little meat bundles deemed them one of Nanny's best dishes—tiny roll-ups of tender veal pounded as thinly as possible, then filled with provolone, herbs, and bread crumbs and griddled on her special griddle. She cooked them one at a time, and they'd disappear instantly to one of the many family members huddled around her cook station. This is one of the recipes that makes me most grateful for my Italian family experiences.

In defense of veal, it's a far more sustainable meat choice than beef, and there are some wonderful, responsible farmers raising it today. In this recipe, where the meat is only lightly seared and not braised at all, there really is no substitute. Be careful not to tear the veal while pounding, and don't be tempted to overfill the delicate *braciolini*. My only other advice: volunteer to do the dishes so you can scrape the bits of toasted cheese off the bottom of the pan.

2 Tbsp plain dried bread crumbs

1 Tbsp finely grated Pecorino Romano cheese

1½ tsp finely chopped garlic

1½ tsp finely chopped fresh Italian parsley leaves

2 Tbsp plus 1½ tsp extra-virgin olive oil

12 oz [340 g] boneless veal cutlets, about 2 large or 4 small cutlets

1½ oz [40 g] provolone cheese, cut into thin slices, then broken into pieces

4 very thin slices prosciutto, cut into strips

Salt

Freshly ground black pepper

4 fresh sage leaves

2 sprigs fresh rosemary, cut into 1- to 2-in [2.5- to 5-cm] pieces

Lemon wedges, for serving (optional)

MAKES 14 TO 16

In a small bowl, add the bread crumbs, Pecorino Romano, garlic, parsley, and 1 Tbsp of olive oil. Stir well to combine. Set aside.

Pound the cutlets (see Sidebar, page 127) to about ¹⁄₁₆ in [2 mm] thick, or as thin as possible without tearing the meat. Trim the pounded cutlets into pieces about 2½ in [6 cm] long and 3 in [7.5 cm] wide. You should have between fourteen and sixteen pieces.

Working with one piece at a time, spread out a piece of veal on your cutting board. Place one or a few very small, narrow pieces of provolone vertically down the center (it should only cover an area slightly smaller than the center of the meat itself). Top the cheese with a small strip of prosciutto (less is more when filling the *braciolini*; don't get carried away). Top with a small amount of the bread crumb mixture [about ¼ tsp], spreading the crumbs in a vertical line atop the prosciutto and cheese. Fold one of the parallel edges of the veal over the filling and continue to roll tightly until the

continued

filling is completely covered and the veal has been wrapped into a neat cylindrical bundle. (The filling should not be hanging out the open ends of the veal bundle; adjust if needed.) Repeat with the remaining veal pieces, leaving a little of the bread crumb mixture behind at the end. Lightly season the veal rolls with salt, then generously season with pepper.

Take out three long wooden skewers. Working one at a time, thread a *braciolini* crosswise onto each skewer (alternatively, use plain wooden toothpicks if you don't have skewers). Follow with a whole sage leaf or 1- to 2-in [2.5- to 5-cm] branch of rosemary. Add another *braciolini* to keep the herb in position. Repeat until you have four to six pieces of *braciolini* on each skewer (you don't have to place an herb between each one). Spread the reserved bread crumb mixture all over the outsides of the meat pieces, patting to adhere.

Heat a large cast-iron or other heavy-bottomed skillet over medium-high heat and add the remaining 1 Tbsp plus 1½ tsp of olive oil. Once hot, carefully add the skewers (break off 1 to 2 in [2.5 to 5 cm] of wood at the end of any skewers that don't fit in the pan). Cook on the first side until well seared, about 4 minutes. Using tongs, turn the skewers and continue cooking until no pink remains on the veal and both sides are well seared, 2 to 3 minutes more.

Remove and serve immediately, squeezed with a little lemon, if desired.

How to Pound Meat

While not difficult, this does take some finessing. Here's how I do it:

1. If the cutlets are large, trim them into more manageable pieces—no wider than the width of three or four fingers and no longer than your hand.

2. Place a large piece of plastic wrap on a flat, stable surface. One at a time, add 1 cutlet to the center of the plastic and cover with a second large piece of plastic wrap.

3. Using the flat side of a meat mallet or something flat with a decently wide surface area (like the bottom of a heavy liquid measuring cup), begin pounding the meat, starting near the center and pulling outward gently and slightly as you pound to help the meat spread thinner and wider on all sides. Repeat until the meat is a uniform thickness, being careful not to tear the flesh.

BRAISED ARTICHOKES

with pistachio pesto and burrata

There are few sounds more beautiful on a Sunday than the purr of something simmering on the stove—which is perfect for artichokes, because, admittedly, it takes a long, slow day for me to justify cleaning and preparing them. In the case of this dish, where you'll be eating the leaves, hearts, and all, you really want to cook them until they're almost as soft as the burrata you'll serve them with.

The best artichokes for eating whole are usually the baby kind, or up to a medium artichoke. But you can use large artichokes here, too (see cover photo), if they're trimmed down to their most tender parts—it may just take some extra fork and finger work to eat them.

ARTICHOKES

1 tsp kosher salt

10 peppercorns

1 garlic clove, peeled and smashed

2 large lemons, halved

2 lb [910 g] artichokes,
about 12 medium-small or 3 large

TOPPINGS

4 oz [115 g] burrata

1 recipe Pistachio Pesto (page 123)

Lemon wedges, for squeezing

Pink peppercorns, crushed,
for garnishing (optional)

SERVES 6 TO 8

In a large pot, combine 6 cups [1.4 L] of water, the salt, peppercorns, and garlic. Squeeze the juice from the 2 lemons into the water, then add the lemon halves and stir.

Cut or tear away the toughest outer leaves of the artichokes. Using scissors, snip off the tips of each remaining artichoke leaf. Peel away the outermost part of the long stems using a vegetable peeler. Using a chef's knife, halve each artichoke lengthwise from tip to stem. Use a spoon to remove the hairy chokes and the fibrous innermost leaves from the center of each half and discard. Transfer the cleaned artichoke halves to the lemon water and repeat.

Bring the water to a simmer and cook until the hearts of the artichokes feel tender when poked with a knife, and the leaves pull away easily from the base, 35 to 40 minutes. Drain the water and discard the aromatics. You can use the artichokes warm now, or serve at room temperature.

Arrange the artichokes on a platter cut-side up. Break the burrata into pieces and distribute among the artichokes. Smear the artichokes with pesto. Squeeze with lemon and sprinkle with pink peppercorns, if desired.

GRILLED LAMB LOIN CHOPS

with red wine vinegar marinade

Lamb is one of the most popular meats in Italy, especially the central and southern parts, and is eaten all over the country during Easter. It's often roasted and, when it is, wine and vinegar are used frequently as seasonings. I love lamb on the grill— it's quick and painless to prepare, and the high heat keeps the insides medium-rare while the outside sears and darkens. I toss it in a red wine vinegar marinade *after* it's cooked, so you can still taste the tart, floral vinegar as you eat.

8 to 12 individual lamb loin chops, or rib chops [1½ to 2 lb, or 680 to 910 g, total], sliced between the bones

1 tsp kosher salt, plus more as needed

Freshly ground black pepper

¼ packed cup [3 g] fresh Italian parsley leaves, coarsely torn

4 garlic cloves, coarsely sliced lengthwise

2 Tbsp extra-virgin olive oil

1 tsp red wine vinegar

Crusty bread, for serving (optional)

SERVES 8 TO 12

Season the lamb chops all over with 1 tsp of salt and some pepper. Rub to adhere. Let the meat sit out at room temperature for about 30 minutes.

Meanwhile, on a rimmed serving platter large enough to fit the lamb, combine the parsley, garlic, olive oil, 2 Tbsp of water, the vinegar, and a pinch each of salt and pepper. Stir briefly to combine. Set aside.

Preheat a grill to medium-high heat. Set the marinade next to the grill.

Transfer the lamb chops to the grill and cook, turning once, until charred on both sides and medium-rare throughout, 4 to 5 minutes total for each. Remove the chops to the platter with the marinade. Using tongs, toss the chops in the mixture to coat. Serve hot or warm, tossing again, if needed, just before serving and with bread for dipping into the juices, if desired.

The Italian creed about making delicious meals by letting simple ingredients shine is never more adhered to than in summer. If you have good olive oil, salt, and a knife—and sometimes a flame—you can make almost any piece of ripe summer produce into an incredible dish for a gathering. That's not to overlook the beautiful briny seafood, grilled meats, and fresh-made fritters and breads that characterize the antipasti table during this season.

While summer recipes tend to be uncomplicated and quick, much of the pleasure of meals in summer comes from the gripping and all-consuming ways we enjoy them: rolling up our sleeves to pluck the sweet seafood from its shells, lapping up the last juices of the grilled meats with bread, or licking the residual grease off our fingers after a crispy vegetable fritter. It's the season to buy, make, and eat a wider variety of foods.

SUMMER

SQUASH BLOSSOM FRITTERS

with fresh basil and pecorino romano

My great-aunt and great-uncle kept a massive vegetable garden beside their house and tended to it well into their nineties. At some point each summer, they'd send us home with a brown paper bag filled with flowers from their zucchini plants. No matter how many we got, it was never enough to fulfill our appetites for them. We'd work them into these crispy fritters, which we simply called "flowers" for short, as they were basically the only way we ever ate the blossoms in our family. The chopped flowers are seasoned lightly with fresh basil and Pecorino, and held together by a little flour before being panfried. The flavor is intense and unadulterated, the true essence of the blossoms. Savor every bite.

5 oz [140 g, or 4 loosely packed cups] zucchini flowers (squash blossoms)

5 Tbsp [40 g] all-purpose flour

¼ packed cup [10 g] chopped fresh basil leaves

1 Tbsp plus 1 tsp finely grated Pecorino Romano cheese

2 generous pinches of kosher salt

2 generous pinches of freshly ground black pepper

3 Tbsp extra-virgin olive oil, plus more as needed

SERVES 4

Finely chop the zucchini flowers (you will have about 2 full cups). Transfer to a medium bowl.

To the bowl, add the flour, 5 Tbsp [75 ml] of water, the basil, cheese, salt, and pepper. Mix well to combine into a thick, moist batter.

Line a plate with paper towels and set it near the stove. In a large nonstick skillet over medium-high heat, heat the olive oil. Once hot, scoop ¼ cup [60 ml] of the batter into the pan (the oil should sizzle significantly). Using the back of a spoon or small spatula, spread out the batter to form a thin pancake. Repeat with more batter, fitting as many fritters as you can in the pan without crowding them. Cook each until one side is deeply browned and crispy looking, 4 to 5 minutes. Carefully flip with a spatula and cook the remaining side for 4 to 5 minutes more. Transfer to the prepared plate. Continue cooking the remaining fritters, adding more olive oil as needed to the pan. Serve hot.

CORNMEAL FRITTERS
with softened herb butter

These crispy cornmeal fritters (*frittelle di mais*) are a fun, crowd-pleasing finger food. You don't need a deep-fryer—any large pot will do. But having a deep-fat thermometer and monitoring the frying temperature help ensure each cooks through in the center before the outside overdarkens. These make big round pieces, sort of like large hushpuppies, flecked with herbs and fresh corn kernels. The orange zest and herb-infused butter is optional; they're great on their own, too. If using, remember to set the butter out at room temperature the moment you begin.

FRITTERS

1½ cups [204 g] yellow cornmeal

½ cup [65 g] unbleached all-purpose flour

2 Tbsp sugar

1½ tsp baking powder

1½ tsp kosher salt,
plus more for sprinkling

1 large egg

⅓ cup [80 ml] plus ¼ cup [60 ml] whole milk

1 cup [140 g] fresh sweet corn kernels

2 Tbsp finely chopped fresh basil leaves

1 Tbsp finely chopped
Italian parsley leaves

1 Tbsp finely chopped shallot

2 medium garlic cloves,
grated on a Microplane

Canola oil, for frying

HERB BUTTER

1 cup [2 sticks, 8 oz, or 226 g] unsalted butter,
at room temperature

2 Tbsp plus 2 tsp finely chopped fresh
Italian parsley leaves

1 Tbsp finely chopped fresh basil

1 Tbsp minced shallot

½ tsp finely grated orange zest

1 tsp honey

¼ tsp kosher salt

MAKES 12 TO 15

MAKE THE FRITTERS: In a medium bowl, combine the cornmeal, flour, sugar, baking powder, and 1½ tsp of salt. Stir well.

In a small bowl, beat the egg with ⅓ cup [80 ml] of milk. Add to the cornmeal mixture and stir to combine.

In a blender, combine the corn kernels and remaining ¼ cup [60 ml] of milk. Process until lightly chunky. Add to the cornmeal mixture. Stir in the basil, parsley, shallot, and garlic until fully combined.

MAKE THE HERB BUTTER: In a small bowl, combine the butter, parsley, basil, shallot, orange zest, honey, and salt. Stir and mash the ingredients together to combine. Cover and set aside at room temperature until ready to serve.

Line a baking sheet with paper towels or a wire drying rack and set it next to the stove.

continued

Pour enough canola oil into an 8-in [20-cm] heavy-bottomed pot that it reaches at least 2 in [5 cm] up the sides of the pot. Set the pot over medium-high heat and let warm until the oil registers just about 350°F [180°C] on a deep-fat thermometer.

Quickly add 1 heaping Tbsp of the cornmeal mixture, keeping the scoop of batter in as much of a ball shape as you can (use a small cookie scoop if you have one). Add 3 or 4 more scoops of batter (you want to cook the fritters in batches without overcrowding the pan). Cook, turning the fritters occasionally with a spider skimmer or slotted spoon, until deeply browned on all sides and just cooked throughout, about 5 minutes. As you cook, adjust the heat to maintain the oil temperature at 350°F [180°C].

Using the slotted spoon or spider, remove the fritters to the prepared baking sheet or rack and immediately sprinkle with salt. Continue to fry the fritters in batches of 4 or 5 until all the batter has been used.

Serve warm with the herb butter for dipping.

CHARRED RADICCHIO AND CORN SALAD

with fennel and yogurt dressing

Like any good Italian, I love bitter greens and vegetables, including radicchio, one of the easiest to find in any grocery store and prettiest to prepare. It's hearty and pungent, but charring the leaves on the grill really mellows the flavor, as does serving this dish with sweet summer corn sliced right from the cob.

You can use this citrusy yogurt, honey, and garlic vinaigrette dressing again and again on any salad with a similar balance of flavors—or just on grilled vegetables.

Leave a little of the radicchio root intact to help keep the pieces in neat wedges for grilling.

2 round heads radicchio [about 1 lb, or 455 g, total], cut through the roots into 12 wedges

4 Tbsp [60 ml] plus 1 tsp extra-virgin olive oil

Kosher salt

2 ears fresh yellow corn, shucked

2 Tbsp full-fat plain yogurt

¼ cup [60 ml] fresh lemon juice

2 Tbsp fresh lime juice

¼ tsp grated garlic

¼ tsp honey

Freshly ground black pepper

½ packed cup [83 g] very thinly sliced fennel, from about ½ medium bulb, plus fennel fronds, for garnishing

Finely chopped chives, for garnishing

Flaky sea salt

SERVES 6

In a large bowl, combine the radicchio wedges and 1 Tbsp plus 1 tsp olive oil. Season with about ⅛ tsp of kosher salt and toss to coat the radicchio.

Preheat a grill to medium-high heat.

Place the radicchio wedges and corn on the grill. Cook, rotating occasionally as needed, until the radicchio is well charred and the corn is lightly charred, 6 to 8 minutes for the radicchio and about 8 minutes for the corn. Remove.

Once slightly cooled, cut the corn from the cob using a sharp knife.

In a medium bowl, whisk the yogurt, lemon juice, lime juice, remaining 3 Tbsp of olive oil, the garlic, honey, a pinch of kosher salt, and a generous amount of pepper to form a dressing. Add half the corn and fennel to the bowl with the dressing and toss briefly to coat. Nestle the radicchio wedges into the dressing, turning them to coat.

In a large, wide, shallow bowl or on a rimmed platter, place the radicchio wedges and the dressed vegetables. Top with the remaining corn and fennel and spoon the remaining dressing on top. Garnish with some fennel fronds, chives, flaky sea salt, and more pepper, and serve.

ROASTED CHERRIES

with sour cream and hazelnuts

Midsummer in Italy is cherry season, and Italians go crazy for them. The beautiful range of colors—black, red, and white—is outshone only by the gorgeous names of the varieties: *Durone, Mora, Malizia, Ferrovia, Amarena,* **and so on. While you'll find them often in jams, in desserts, or preserved in alcohol, this rendering features them in a savory way, roasted in vinegar and served alongside sour cream and toasted nuts. Let them cool slightly so the cream has a better chance to adhere. And warn guests to watch out for the pits, which are left intact during roasting.**

1 Tbsp red wine vinegar

1 tsp extra-virgin olive oil

1 tsp honey

⅛ tsp kosher salt

Freshly ground black pepper

24 [about 8 oz, or 230 g] sweet red cherries, stems intact

½ cup [120 g] sour cream

2 Tbsp chopped roasted hazelnuts

SERVES 6

See photo page 142

Preheat the oven to 400°F [200°C].

Meanwhile, in a medium bowl, combine the vinegar, olive oil, honey, salt, and a little pepper. Stir with a fork to combine. Add the cherries and toss well to coat.

Transfer the cherries to a small parchment paper–lined rimmed baking sheet, reserving the remaining dressing in the bowl.

Roast the cherries until the juices are running and the flesh has mostly collapsed, 18 to 20 minutes. Remove and let cool slightly in the pan.

Carefully transfer the cherries to a serving bowl, shifting them largely to one side of the bowl. Drizzle with a little of the reserved dressing. On the free side of the bowl, dollop the sour cream. Sprinkle the fruit and cream with the hazelnuts and serve.

Marinated Blackberries and
Cantaloupe with Citrus, Shallot,
Fish Sauce, and Mint (page 144)

Roasted Cherries with
Sour Cream and Hazelnuts
(page 140)

Nectarine, Salami, and Arugula Salad with Cinnamon and Chili (page 145)

Fresh Peach and Cucumber Salad with Dried Chili Oil (page 145)

GRILLED APRICOTS

with pistachio pesto and sea salt

Sweet stone fruits are a welcome addition to any antipasti spread, but oh, how much better the fruit tastes grilled and slathered in pesto. Be sure the grill is very hot so the outside of the fruit caramelizes.

6 firm-ripe apricots,
halved lengthwise and pitted

Extra-virgin olive oil, for brushing

Kosher salt

1 recipe Pistachio Pesto (page 123)

Flaky sea salt, for garnishing

Finely grated lemon zest,
for garnishing (optional)

Crème fraîche, for serving

SERVES 6

Preheat a grill or grill pan to high heat. Be sure the grate is brushed clean.

Brush the cut sides of the apricots with olive oil and season lightly with kosher salt.

Place the apricots cut-side down on the grill grate and cook, checking occasionally, until grill marks appear, 2 to 3 minutes. Using tongs or a spatula, rotate the pieces 90 degrees and cook 1 to 2 minutes more. Transfer the apricots cut-side up to a platter and let cool slightly.

Dollop or smear with some of the pistachio pesto and sprinkle with flaky sea salt and more olive oil or lemon zest, if desired. Serve warm, with crème fraîche on the side.

MARINATED BLACKBERRIES AND CANTALOUPE

with citrus, shallot, fish sauce, and mint

The Italians have been known to hide subtle fishy flavorings in dishes, usually by pulverizing an anchovy into a sauce or dressing, or using a concentrated liquid called *colatura* they make from aging anchovy juices. I find both of these a little overpowering for fresh fruit, but I do like using a dash of Asian-style fish sauce to give sweet fruit salad some subtle complexity.

2 pints [1½ lb, or 680 g] fresh blackberries

⅛ small cantaloupe [about 3½ oz, or 100 g],
very thinly sliced into ribbons [about 1 cup]

2 tsp minced shallot

1 Tbsp plus 1 tsp cane sugar

¼ cup [60 ml] fresh lime juice

1 tsp fish sauce

Kosher salt

Freshly ground black pepper

Finely chopped fresh mint or cilantro,
for serving (optional)

SERVES 4

In a medium serving bowl, combine the black-berries and the cantaloupe slices. Sprinkle the shallot and sugar onto the fruit, and stir to coat. Drizzle the lime juice and fish sauce on top. Season the mixture with a small pinch each of salt and pepper and stir gently to coat. Sprinkle with the herbs, if using, and serve.

See photo page 142

FRESH PEACH AND CUCUMBER SALAD

with dried chili oil

Fruit makes a lovely light first bite or accent to a meal. This mixture of luscious, fragrant peaches is brought into the savory realm with chilled cucumbers and a touch of dried chili oil.

7 oz [200 g] mini seedless, Persian, or English cucumber

2 firm-ripe peaches [14 oz, or 400 g, total], pitted and sliced into wedges

1 Tbsp plus 1 tsp extra-virgin olive oil

1 Tbsp Dried Chili Oil, for drizzling (page 30)

¼ tsp flaky sea salt

Freshly ground black pepper

SERVES 4

Using a vegetable peeler, partially peel the cucumbers in strips, removing about half the total peel of each cucumber. Discard the peel. Halve the cucumbers lengthwise, then slice them about ½ in [12 mm] thick on the diagonal (you will have about 1½ cups).

In a medium shallow serving bowl, combine the cucumbers and the peach wedges. Toss gently to mix. When ready to serve, drizzle the mixture with the olive oil. Using a spoon, drizzle on some of the chili oil liquids and solids, erring on the conservative side. Sprinkle the salad with flaky sea salt and a little black pepper and serve immediately.

See photo page 143

NECTARINE, SALAMI, AND ARUGULA SALAD

with cinnamon and chili

Handfuls of spicy arugula greens, slices of salty and fatty salami, and a pinch of smoky cinnamon counteract the nectary flavors of the fruit.

3 Tbsp extra-virgin olive oil

2 Tbsp red wine vinegar

2 Tbsp thinly sliced shallot

Kosher salt

Freshly ground black pepper

4 packed cups [4 oz, or 115 g] arugula

2 firm-ripe white or yellow nectarines, pitted and thinly sliced [1½ cups]

3 oz [85 g] dried salami link, such as soppressata, thinly sliced, then halved, if desired

1 to 2 pinches of ground cinnamon

Chili flakes (optional)

SERVES 6

In a large bowl, whisk the olive oil, vinegar, shallot, and a generous pinch each of salt and pepper. Add the arugula and toss to coat in the dressing. Add the nectarines and salami pieces and toss briefly and gently to combine.

Gently transfer the salad to a platter or serve straight from the mixing bowl. Sprinkle the top with a pinch or two of cinnamon, some chili flakes, if desired, and salt and pepper. Serve immediately.

See photo page 143

OLIVE OIL CORNMEAL CAKE

with rosemary and honey

Made with a dash each of vanilla, honey, and butter-milk, this cornmeal and flour batter produces a lightly sweet, moist but crumbly cake. Traditionally in Italy, cakes like this were often baked with lard and studded with cut grapes, raisins, or pine nuts. Once out of the oven, this version is brushed with more olive oil and topped with rosemary—also traditional—releasing an herbaceous, fruity perfume.

CAKE

1 cup [136 g] cornmeal

1 cup [130 g] unbleached all-purpose flour

1½ tsp kosher salt

½ tsp baking powder

¼ tsp baking soda

5 Tbsp [2½ oz, or 70 g] unsalted butter

5 Tbsp [75 ml] fruity extra-virgin olive oil

⅓ cup [65 g] sugar

1 Tbsp plus 1 tsp honey

3 large eggs

¼ tsp pure vanilla extract

¾ cup [180 ml] whole milk

½ cup [120 ml] buttermilk

GARNISH

1 Tbsp extra-virgin olive oil

Fresh rosemary [about 2 Tbsp], or crumbled chive flowers or fresh thyme

Flaky sea salt

Freshly ground black pepper

SERVES 8 TO 10

MAKE THE CAKE: Preheat the oven to 400°F [200°C].

Meanwhile, in a medium bowl, add the cornmeal, flour, salt, baking powder, and baking soda. Whisk briefly to combine.

In a small saucepan over medium-low heat, melt 4 Tbsp [56 g] of butter. Pour the butter into a large heat-proof bowl and let cool slightly. Add 4 Tbsp [60 ml] of olive oil, the sugar, and honey. Whisk in the eggs and vanilla until incorporated. Whisk in the milk and buttermilk until incorporated. Gradually add the cornmeal mixture, stirring the batter with a spatula until mostly smooth.

Set a 9-in [23-cm] cake pan in the oven with the remaining 1 Tbsp each of butter and olive oil in it. Once the butter melts, remove the pan and tilt it until the bottom and a little of the sides are coated with the fats.

Stir the cornmeal batter well and pour it into the hot pan. Spread to fill evenly. Bake until golden brown in places and a tester inserted into the center comes out clean, 22 to 25 minutes.

TO GARNISH THE CAKE: Brush with the olive oil and sprinkle with the rosemary, lots of flaky sea salt, and a little pepper. Let cool slightly. Cut into wedges or squares and serve hot or warm for best results. (It's also perfectly good at room temperature.) Once cooled, store in an airtight container or wrapped tightly with plastic wrap for up to 4 days.

CHILLED MUSSELS SALAD

with celery, leek, and parsley

I like to put out a little bowl of these pickle-y mussels as I would olives—right next to a charcuterie board or alongside warm crispy toasts, bread, or crackers with wine. Plucked from their shells and tossed with a lemony dressing and some celery and cooked leek, they're more like a condiment or accessory than a meal in themselves. They're best made a few hours or a day ahead so they have time to chill properly.

1 Tbsp red wine vinegar

Freshly ground black pepper

2 large garlic cloves, minced

2 lb [910 g] small mussels,
rinsed and cleaned under cool water

1 medium [6-oz, or 170-g] leek, trimmed, halved
lengthwise, and sliced 1/3 in [8 mm] thick (1³/₄ cups)

2 Tbsp extra-virgin olive oil

½ cup [60 g] thinly sliced celery,
from about 1 trimmed inner stalk,
leaves coarsely torn

1 Tbsp fresh lemon juice

Kosher salt

Grilled Crostini (page 39)
or other bread, for serving (optional)

SERVES 4

See photo page 147

In a medium saucepan, combine ¾ cup [180 ml] of water, the vinegar, a pinch of pepper, and half the minced garlic. Bring to a strong simmer over high heat. Add the mussels and cover the pan. Cook, shaking the pan occasionally, until the mussels open, 4 to 5 minutes. Remove from the heat.

Set the juices aside to cool. Pluck the mussels from the shells (discard any that did not open). Discard the shells, and add the mussels back to the cooled juices. Cover and refrigerate until ready to eat, up to 1 day.

Bring the mussels out of the refrigerator about 15 minutes before serving.

Transfer the leeks to a strainer and rinse in cool water, breaking up the pieces with your fingers, until clear of dirt and sand. Let drain slightly.

In a large skillet over medium-high heat, heat 1 Tbsp of olive oil. Add the leeks and the remaining minced garlic. Cook, stirring until the leeks are softened, 8 to 10 minutes. Turn off the heat and stir in the sliced celery.

In a serving bowl, combine the remaining 1 Tbsp of olive oil, the lemon juice, and a pinch each of salt and pepper. Add the mussels (discard their juices). Stir well. Add the celery and leek mixture and a pinch each of salt and pepper. Toss to coat. Serve with crostini or bread, if desired.

ROMAN "TRECCIA" BREADS

with mozzarella, salami, and garlic scapes

In Rome, you'll find a traditional *treccia* (braid) shape used in handmade mozzarella, as well as in the occasional bakery bread. Often these breads are filled with salty and sweet morsels, from olives to cubed salumi to pine nuts or dried fruits. Here in this twisted instead of braided version, I use finely diced salami, mozzarella, and crunchy green garlic scapes, which you can find at most farmers' markets and some gourmet stores during the summer. They have all the robust flavor of fresh garlic but without as much of its spicy sting. If you can't find them, substitute sliced scallion or a flavorful, hearty chopped green olive such as Castelvetrano, patted dry before using.

1 lb [455 g] good-quality pizza dough, at room temperature

½ cup [about 3 oz, or 85 g] finely cubed dried salami

1 large or 2 medium garlic scapes [¾ oz, or 20 g, total], thinly sliced

½ cup [about 3½ oz, or 100 g] finely diced fresh mozzarella cheese

Kosher salt

Freshly ground black pepper

3 Tbsp extra-virgin olive oil

MAKES 4; SERVES 8 TO 12

Preheat the oven to 425°F [220°C] and set a rack in the top third of the oven. If you have a pizza stone, baking steel, or sturdy large metal baking sheet (though you'll need a second one for baking the breads), preheat that, too. Line a baking sheet with parchment paper and set aside.

Meanwhile, cut the dough into four equal strips [4 oz, or 115 g, each]. One at a time and working on a clean, unfloured counter as needed, stretch and roll (using a rolling pin) a piece of pizza dough into a 14- to 16-in- [35.5- to 40.5-cm-] long strip about 3 in [7.5 cm] wide. If the dough springs back too much between rolling, let it rest on the counter for 3 to 5 minutes and resume.

Once stretched, pick up the dough off the counter and set it back down to make sure it's not sticking too firmly. Spread one-fourth of the salami cubes, sliced garlic scapes, and mozzarella down one long side of the dough, distributing them relatively evenly. Pat the pieces gently to adhere them to the dough. Season lightly all over with salt and pepper. Then, starting from one of the long sides, roll the clean side of the dough around the filling, pressing and pinching the long ends together to seal. Pinch the short ends to seal in the filling completely.

continued

Transfer to the parchment paper–lined baking sheet (the pieces will be 10 to 12 in, or 25 to 30.5 cm, long now). Holding on to the short ends of the dough, spin the dough ends in opposite directions to form a tight, long twist. You can stretch the dough gently as you twist to be sure the pieces stay long and thin. Place the twist back on the baking sheet and repeat rolling, filling, and twisting the remaining dough pieces.

Brush the pieces all over with about 1 Tbsp of olive oil and season lightly with salt. Transfer to the oven. If you're using a baking stone or baking steel, add as many dough twists to the preheated surface as you can without them touching one another. If you are using a second baking sheet (and have one preheating in the oven), space all the dough pieces on the cool baking sheet so they are not touching. Transfer to the oven, placing the cool baking sheet on top of the hot one, and bake until the breads just start to brown, 15 to 20 minutes. Open the oven and quickly brush with the remaining 2 Tbsp of olive oil. Bake until golden brown all over, 8 to 10 minutes more.

Remove and let cool slightly before serving.

SHRIMP AND CHERRY TOMATO FRA DIAVOLO

with bacon and fresh corn

They say *fra diavolo* sauce may be an Italian-American invention, and that it migrated backward to Italy. Typically you'll see a version of this spicy red sauce—often made with garlic, oregano, and sometimes a little booze—on the pasta section of menus, where it's usually served with linguini or spaghetti and a mix of shellfish such as lobster, shrimp, clams, or mussels. This is my antipasto version, made deliberately less saucy, without pasta, and with fresh (not just canned) summer tomatoes and corn. I like mine extra spicy, with near double this amount of crushed chili flakes added. That's what chilled wine is for.

18 extra-large shrimp, shelled and deveined, tails on if desired

Kosher salt

Freshly ground black pepper

2 Tbsp extra-virgin olive oil

1 bacon slice or pancetta slice [1 to 2 oz, or 30 to 55 g], finely chopped

½ medium yellow onion [3 oz, or 100 g], finely chopped (½ cup plus 2 Tbsp)

4 garlic cloves, minced

1 cup [240 ml] dry white wine

1 cup [242 g] canned crushed tomatoes and their juices

1 cup [about 6 oz, or 170 g] quartered fresh yellow or red cherry tomatoes

1 tsp finely chopped fresh basil leaves, plus more for serving

¼ tsp chili flakes, plus more as desired

½ cup [70 g] fresh corn kernels

Crusty bread, for serving

SERVES 4 TO 6

Season the shrimp lightly with salt and pepper. In a medium saucepan over medium-high heat, heat the olive oil. Once hot, add the shrimp. Cook, turning as needed, until lightly seared and just cooked through, 3 to 5 minutes total. Transfer to a plate and reserve.

Add the bacon to the hot pan. Cook, stirring, until crispy, about 3 minutes. Add the onion and season lightly with salt. Cook, stirring occasionally, until softened, 2 minutes. Stir in the garlic and cook until fragrant, about 1 minute more. Add the wine and cook until reduced by about half, about 4 minutes. Add the crushed tomatoes and cherry tomatoes, the basil, chili flakes, and a pinch each of salt and pepper. Bring to a low simmer. Lower the heat to maintain a low simmer and cook, stirring occasionally, until a thick sauce forms and the cherry tomatoes begin to soften, about 12 minutes. Stir in the corn and cook for 30 seconds. Add the shrimp back to the pan and stir to coat with the sauce.

Transfer to a serving dish and garnish with more basil and more chili flakes to taste. Serve warm with crusty bread.

TOMATO, RAW BEET, AND STRAWBERRY PANZANELLA

with cucumbers and shallots

In the past, Tuscans were said to bake fresh bread only every few days, which meant that many of their bread-based dishes were derived from loaves several days old. Panzanella is a well-known salad that makes good use of them, the stale bread cubes coming back to life from soaking up the sweet juices of the tomatoes. This one also contains crunchy raw beets and sweet strawberries. Use a hearty loaf of white or whole-wheat bread—fresh or day-old—that holds together well when diced.

TOASTED BREAD

3 Tbsp extra-virgin olive oil

3 cups [about 8 oz, or 230 g] cubed [¾ in, or 2 cm] country Italian bread or baguette

¼ tsp kosher salt

SALAD

3 medium raw beets [about 1 lb or 455 g], peeled using a vegetable peeler

1 large and 1 medium firm-ripe heirloom tomatoes [1 lb 5 oz, or 595 g, total], preferably a mix of colors and varieties, sliced into wedges [4 cups]

1½ pints [15 oz, or 455 g] cherry tomatoes, preferably a mix of colors and varieties, halved through the stem sides [3 cups]

1 medium [about 8 oz, or 230 g] cucumber, halved lengthwise and thinly sliced [1¼ cups]

1 cup [140 g] thinly sliced ripe strawberries

¼ cup [60 ml] extra-virgin olive oil

¼ cup [60 ml] red wine vinegar

1 Tbsp minced shallot

Kosher salt

Freshly ground black pepper

Fresh basil leaves, for garnishing

SERVES 8 TO 10

TOAST THE BREAD: In a large skillet over medium heat, add the olive oil. Once hot, add the bread and stir to coat. Sprinkle with the salt and cook, stirring occasionally, until well toasted and crispy, 6 to 8 minutes. Transfer to a large plate.

PREPARE THE SALAD: Slice the beets into ¼-in- [6-mm-] thick rounds. Then thinly slice each round to create 1-in- [2.5-cm-] long and ¼-in- [6-mm-] thick sticks (you will have about 2 cups). Place the beets in a large bowl and add the heirloom tomatoes, cherry tomatoes, cucumbers, and strawberries.

In a small bowl, combine the olive oil, vinegar, and shallot. Season with a pinch each of salt and pepper and whisk well to combine. Pour the dressing over the salad and toss briefly and gently to coat. The salad can sit for up to 1 hour before serving. Do not add the bread until ready to serve.

When ready to serve, stir half the bread pieces into the mixture. Transfer the salad to a serving platter, top with basil leaves, the remaining pieces of bread, and a sprinkling of salt and pepper and serve.

HEIRLOOM TOMATO CROSTATA

with basil, garlic, and shallot

In Italy, a *crostata* is a rustic, open-face tart, most often a fruit filling surrounded by a flaky crust. This is a savory version, with salt and pepper in the pastry dough, ripe summer tomatoes, and delicate notes of garlic, shallot, and fresh basil. While you can eat this at room temperature anytime the day it's baked, the buttery crust will taste the freshest and remain the most crisp within 30 minutes or so after pulling it from the oven—something to consider when timing your baking.

DOUGH

1¼ cups plus 1 tsp unbleached all-purpose flour [162 g], plus more for rolling the dough

1½ tsp sugar

¼ tsp kosher salt

⅛ tsp freshly ground black pepper

½ cup [1 stick, or 113 g] very cold unsalted butter, cut into ½-in [12-mm] cubes

4 to 5 Tbsp [60 to 75 ml] ice-cold water

1 large egg, beaten

TOMATO FILLING

3 medium heirloom tomatoes [about 1¼ lb, or 570 g, total], preferably multicolor

1½ tsp minced shallot

¾ tsp minced garlic

1 loosely packed tsp chopped fresh basil or whole basil flowers

¼ tsp sea salt or kosher salt

1 Tbsp unsalted butter, sliced or broken into small pieces

SERVES 8

MAKE THE DOUGH: In a food processor or large bowl, mix 1¼ cups [162 g] of flour, the sugar, salt, and pepper until just combined. Add the butter and either pulse using the machine or work it in using a pastry cutter or your fingers until only pea-size crumbs remain. Add 4 Tbsp [60 ml] of ice-cold water, pulsing or mixing with a fork or pastry cutter until the mixture is crumbly and holds together easily when pinched. Only if needed to bring the dough together, mix in 1 Tbsp more ice-cold water.

Turn out the mixture onto a large piece of plastic wrap. Using the sides of the plastic and the warmth and pressure from your hands, pack the mixture together tightly until you can form it into a compact circular disk about 1 in [2.5 cm] tall with no cracks or crumbles inside the plastic wrap. Reposition the wrap to seal the dough tightly and refrigerate for 1 hour, or up to 1 day.

MAKE THE CROSTATA: Position a rack in the center of the oven and preheat the oven to 425°F [220°C].

Slice the tomatoes ¼ in [6 mm] thick and let some of the excess moisture drain off; reserve the juices in a small bowl.

continued

Line a large baking sheet with parchment paper and set it in the refrigerator. On a well-floured work surface (or on a large piece of parchment paper if you're afraid of the dough sticking), use a rolling pin to roll out the dough into a thin, about 12-in- [30.5-cm-] diameter round, adding more flour beneath or atop the dough and spinning it on the floured surface as needed to keep it from sticking. Transfer the dough to the chilled baking sheet (I do this by wrapping my dough around my rolling pin and carefully transferring, then unraveling, it). Line the center of the dough with the remaining 1 tsp of flour, spreading it to coat the part of the dough beneath where the tomatoes will lie.

Add the tomatoes, overlapping them as needed and leaving at least 1½ in [4 cm] of dough bare around the perimeter. Sprinkle on top and in between the layers with the shallot, garlic, and ½ tsp of basil. Wrap the border of the dough carefully over and around the edges of the tomato mixture to form a crust. Place the baking sheet back in the refrigerator for 10 minutes, or the freezer for 5.

Remove and brush the edges of the dough with the beaten egg. Top the center of the tart with the butter pieces. Bake until the dough is golden brown and the bottom of the pastry has set firmly, 40 to 45 minutes. Remove the pan from the oven, and drizzle the center of the tart with some of the reserved tomato juices. Let rest until just warm. Sprinkle with the remaining ½ tsp of fresh basil and the salt and serve sliced into wedges.

CHILLED SEAFOOD SALAD

with parsley and lemon

Insalata di mare is a classic antipasto served in many parts of coastal Italy, especially the south, where you might see it with any mix of seafood including prawns, octopus, mussels, or *scungilli* (conch). It is one of my family's, and many Italian family's, favorites to serve on Christmas Eve. But its quick cooking time and light, lemony dressing make it a delicious idea for summer as well. The celery is almost as essential as the fish, giving the salad freshness, crunch, and contrast and a natural complementary saltiness. Adding the little bay scallops in this version was an idea inspired by my lifelong friends, the Marini family. If you can't find the little bay scallops, avoid substituting with sea scallops; just omit them from the recipe.

1 lb [455 g] calamari,
a mix of tentacles and bodies, cleaned well

1½ lb [680 g] extra-large shrimp,
shelled and deveined, tails left on if desired

4 oz [115 g] small bay scallops, cleaned

1 cup [120 g] finely chopped celery

¼ cup [60 ml] fresh lemon juice, or more to taste

3 Tbsp finely chopped fresh Italian parsley leaves

2 Tbsp extra-virgin olive oil

2 large garlic cloves, peeled

Kosher salt

Freshly ground black pepper

SERVES 6 TO 8

Using a sharp knife, slice the calamari bodies crosswise into thin rings. Store these separately from the tentacles.

Set a medium-large pot full of water to boil over high heat. Once the water boils, set a large bowl of ice water next to the stove. Add the cleaned shrimp to the boiling water and cook until curled and pink, 1 to 2 minutes. Using a slotted spoon or spider, transfer the shrimp to the bowl of ice water.

Add the scallops to the boiling water. Cook for 1½ minutes. With the slotted spoon, transfer to the ice water.

Be sure the water is back up to a boil. Add just the calamari rings to the boiling water and cook until firm, 2 minutes. Transfer to the ice water.

Add the calamari tentacles to the boiling water and cook until firm, 2 minutes. Transfer to the ice water. Discard the cooking water.

Drain all the seafood well from the ice water. Once well drained, cover and refrigerate until chilled, or up to 1 day.

When ready to serve, remove the seafood from the refrigerator. Add the celery, lemon juice, parsley, olive oil, garlic, and a generous pinch each of salt and pepper. Stir well to combine. Taste and adjust the seasoning as needed, adding more lemon juice, salt, or pepper, if desired. Serve immediately.

BLACKENED SUMMER SQUASH

with buttermilk cream sauce, rosemary, and chives

I find summer squash, like pasta, most enjoyable when it's served al dente. The idea here is using high heat on your grill or grill pan to let the squash pieces blacken significantly while still retaining some of their bite. Made with buttermilk and clotted cream, which you can find refrigerated in the specialty section of many grocery stores, the tangy but rich dressing is one you'll want to—and can—put on every vegetable you grill.

¼ cup [60 ml] buttermilk

¼ cup [60 g] clotted cream (available in small jars in the dairy or specialty section)

1¼ tsp fresh rosemary leaves, coarsely chopped, plus more sprigs for garnishing

Kosher salt

6 small to medium summer squash [about 2 lb, or 910 g, total], halved lengthwise, thick ones quartered

Extra-virgin olive oil, for drizzling

2 Tbsp coarsely chopped fresh chives

Smoked sea salt (optional)

SERVES 4 TO 6

Preheat a grill to high heat.

Meanwhile, in a small bowl, whisk the buttermilk, clotted cream, rosemary leaves, and a generous pinch of kosher salt until well combined.

Drizzle the prepared squash lightly with olive oil and season all over with ¼ tsp of kosher salt, rubbing to coat evenly. Transfer the squash to the grill and cook, turning sparingly, until firm-tender and well blackened on both sides, 3 to 4 minutes per side (this may take longer if you're using an indoor grill pan). The squash should be deeply blackened and al dente throughout. Once cooked, transfer to a large platter with the cut sides facing up.

Spoon some or all of the buttermilk dressing over the top of the squash. Sprinkle with the chives and smoked sea salt (if using), and garnish the platter with a few small rosemary sprigs. Serve with any extra sauce on the side.

SAUSAGE-STUFFED FRESH CHERRY PEPPERS

with cheese and bread crumbs

Bite-size spicy-sweet cherry peppers are a designated antipasti pepper in Italy. You'll often see them oil-preserved (see page 21) or marinated and then stuffed with cured meats, cheeses, or tuna fish. The peppers, which are sporadically very spicy but usually more of a medium heat, are even better served warm with a little blistering from the broiler. Because, as an Italian American, you can't think pepper without thinking sausage, I fill them with pork sausage padded with garlic and parsley, and top them with cheesy bread crumbs for toasting under the broiler's heat.

18 medium red cherry peppers [about 14 oz, or 400 g, total]

8 oz [230 g] mild Italian sausage, casings removed

1 tsp minced fresh garlic

1 Tbsp finely chopped fresh Italian parsley leaves, plus more for garnishing

3 Tbsp plus 1 tsp dried bread crumbs

1½ tsp olive oil

⅛ tsp kosher salt

2 packed Tbsp freshly grated Pecorino Romano cheese, grated on a Microplane

Freshly ground black pepper

MAKES 18

See photo page 171

Preheat the oven to 400°F [200°C] and set a rack in the top third of the oven.

Using a paring knife, carefully cut out the stems of the cherry peppers. Using a ¼-tsp measuring spoon or your fingers, scoop out the seeds. (If using your fingers, wash them thoroughly afterward.)

In a medium bowl, combine the sausage, garlic, and 1 Tbsp of parsley. Mix with your fingers to combine.

Fill the peppers with the sausage mixture, ending just shy of the rim of each pepper. (You can refrigerate the filled, uncooked peppers for up to 1 day.) Place the filled peppers on a rimmed baking sheet and cover.

In a small bowl, mix the bread crumbs, olive oil, and salt, tossing with your fingers until fully incorporated. Toss with the cheese and then pack the bread crumb mixture into the tops of the peppers, pressing to fill and adhere.

Bake until the bread crumbs start to brown, 20 minutes. Raise the heat to broil and continue cooking until the bread crumbs are browned and crispy and the peppers are darkened in places, 4 to 6 minutes.

Remove and let cool slightly. Transfer to a rimmed plate or shallow bowl and garnish generously with finely chopped parsley and black pepper before serving.

SEARED ITALIAN SAUSAGES

with roasted cherry tomatoes and shallots

I have this memory of my grandma making sausage. She took out a round cake pan and placed one of those long, coiled herbed sausages into the center, then sprinkled a few slices of potato around it and placed it in the oven to roast. That was it—no garnishes, no frills. It was beautiful and delicious, bronzed and swimming in its own juices in the flimsy metal pan.

My recipe has a few more frills, like fresh basil leaves and on-the-vine cherry tomatoes, and I like to sear the sausages on the stovetop to get them extra crispy. Yet, this recipe is equally effortless and simple. It feels perfectly Italian in that way, served straight from the pan with bread for dipping.

3 pints [about 2½ lb, or 1.2 kg] ripe cherry tomatoes, some left on the vine if desired

4 small shallots [about 6¼ ounces, or 175 g, total], peeled and halved lengthwise

8 garlic cloves, in their skins

2 Tbsp plus 2 tsp extra-virgin olive oil

¼ tsp kosher salt

Freshly ground black pepper

3 Tbsp cold unsalted butter, thinly sliced

4 to 6 hot or mild Italian sausage links [1¼ to 2 lb, or 570 to 910 g, total]

Fresh basil leaves, for garnishing (optional)

Crusty bread, for serving

SERVES 4 TO 8

See photo page 164–65

Preheat the oven to 400°F [200°C].

In a 9-by-13-in [23-by-33-cm] baking dish, scatter the tomatoes, shallots, and garlic cloves. Drizzle with 2 Tbsp of olive oil and sprinkle with the salt and a few pinches of pepper. Top with the butter pieces, distributing them around the pan.

Bake until the tomatoes are wrinkled and some juices have started to pool in the pan, 25 to 30 minutes.

Meanwhile, pierce the sausages in a place or two with a paring knife to allow some of the juices to escape while cooking. In a medium or large skillet over medium heat, add the remaining 2 tsp of olive oil and the sausages. Cook, turning the sausages occasionally, until well seared on all sides and cooked through, 20 to 25 minutes.

Remove the tomatoes and stir briefly. Transfer the sausages to the pan with the tomatoes, nestling them in slightly. Drizzle with the sausage juices, if desired. Garnish with basil leaves (if using) and serve with crusty bread.

SEARED TENDERLOIN CARPACCIO

with dijon, caper, and anchovy sauce

I sear this tenderloin first for some contrast in flavor and color, and fan the pieces around a platter before bathing them in caper sauce. This dish shouldn't sit out too long, which is good, because once in front of guests, it's not likely to last.

BEEF TENDERLOIN

12 oz [340 g] beef tenderloin

Scant ½ tsp kosher salt

¼ tsp freshly ground black pepper

1 Tbsp canola oil

DIJON, CAPER, AND ANCHOVY SAUCE

1 oil-packed anchovy fillet, finely chopped

1 Tbsp plus ½ tsp capers, and 1 tsp caper brine, from the jar

2 tsp white wine vinegar

1 tsp Dijon mustard

1 Tbsp plus 1 tsp extra-virgin olive oil

½ tsp very finely chopped fresh mint

Flaky sea salt

SERVES 4 TO 6

MAKE THE BEEF TENDERLOIN: Rub the beef all over with the salt and pepper. Using a few pieces of butcher twine, tie the tenderloin tightly crosswise every 2 in [5 cm] to create an even shape. Let rest at room temperature for 30 minutes to 1 hour.

Drape a large piece of plastic wrap over a large plate (this is for wrapping the tenderloin after cooking) and set aside.

In a large cast-iron or stainless steel skillet over medium-high heat, heat the canola oil. Once very hot, add the beef (it should sizzle dramatically). Cook undisturbed for 4 minutes. Using tongs, rotate the beef and cook, continuing to rotate as needed, until all sides are well seared, 10 to 12 minutes total. (The beef should be well seared on the outside and very rare on the inside.) Remove and transfer to the plastic wrap. Cover completely with the wrap and seal tightly with a second piece. Set the beef aside to continue "cooking" a little more in its wrappings while you prepare the sauce.

MAKE THE DIJON, CAPER, AND ANCHOVY SAUCE: In a small bowl, add the anchovy, capers, brine, vinegar, mustard, and oil. Mix to combine. Taste and adjust the seasoning as necessary.

Once slightly cooled, unwrap the beef and cut it in half lengthwise. If the pieces are very wide, consider halving them lengthwise again. Using a sharp knife, very thinly slice each piece into thin pieces and distribute them on a large flat serving plate, bringing the cut, seared corners together to form little circular disks. Drizzle with the sauce, then sprinkle with the mint and sea salt to taste; serve immediately.

GRILLED OR BROILED HOT AND SWEET PEPPERS

with mozzarella

I'm so bored by caprese, the overhyped chilled mozzarella and tomato salad. But I never get tired of this delicious replacement, which uses a combination of blackened and raw as well as sweet and spicy peppers. The heat from this dish can vary drastically depending on the type of fresh chiles you buy. So, consider cutting especially spicy peppers into smaller pieces and using less of them. But I love it hot—with the vinegary brine from the jar of pickled *peperoncini* poured all over the top. In a pinch, substitute jarred roasted red peppers, drained of their juices.

2 red bell peppers

2 yellow bell peppers

3 Tbsp extra-virgin olive oil

Kosher salt

Coarsely ground black pepper

6 oz [170 g] fresh mozzarella cheese, coarsely torn or sliced into large pieces [about 1¼ cups]

1 or 2 colorful cherry peppers or other medium-hot chiles, such as jalapeño, seeded and very thinly sliced

2 large pickled peperoncini, drained and thinly sliced, plus some juice from the jar

SERVES 6 TO 8

Preheat a grill to medium-high heat or prepare a broiler and place a rack in the top third of the oven.

If grilling, place the bell peppers on the grate and cook, turning with tongs as needed, until blackened slightly on all sides and just tender, about 10 minutes total. If broiling, place the peppers on a small aluminum foil–lined baking sheet and transfer to the top third of the oven. Broil the peppers, turning with tongs as needed, until blackened slightly on all sides and just tender, about 20 minutes total.

Transfer the bell peppers to a bowl and tent tightly with plastic wrap until cool enough to handle.

Peel about three-fourths of the blackened skin off the peppers, rubbing with your fingers or a clean paper towel to remove it. Remove and discard the stems and seeds as well. Slice the pepper flesh into thick strips.

Drizzle a large serving platter with 1 Tbsp of olive oil. Season the oil lightly with salt. Add the cooked peppers (either warm or at room temperature), and season lightly with salt and black pepper.

Nestle the mozzarella pieces among the peppers, then distribute the fresh chile slices on top. Add the peperoncini. Drizzle the whole dish with the remaining 2 Tbsp of olive oil and 2 to 3 tsp of the brine from the peperoncini jar. Sprinkle with more black pepper and serve.

GRILLED SHELL-ON SHRIMP

with parsley and ginger salmoriglio

Olio all'aglio, the beautiful Italian way of saying "freshly made garlic oil," is a dressing and marinade used on many foods in Italy. I drench meaty fresh shrimp in it before tossing them on the grill and letting the shells char and blister. Once cooked, I toss with an extra-herby *salmoriglio*, another easy dressing traditionally made with chopped parsley, oil, and lemon.

Much of a shrimp's flavor lies in its shell, especially when it takes on all the charred flavors from the grill. So, while you can serve these shrimp peel-and-eat style, consider encouraging guests to crunch through the shrimp whole—shell and all—like I do. Serve them with forks and steak knives, if desired.

6 Tbsp [90 ml] extra-virgin olive oil

3 garlic cloves, minced

Kosher salt

1 lb [455 g] shell-on, wild, extra-large (16 to 20 count) shrimp

¼ cup [10 g] finely chopped fresh Italian parsley leaves

2 tsp fresh lemon juice or red wine vinegar

1 tsp minced shallot

¼ tsp finely grated, fresh peeled ginger, grated on a Microplane

Freshly ground black pepper

Chili flakes, for serving (optional)

SERVES 4

In a small bowl, combine the olive oil, garlic, and ⅛ tsp of salt. Stir.

In a medium bowl, combine the shrimp and half the garlic-oil mixture. Toss well to coat. Set aside until ready to grill.

To the remaining garlic-oil mixture, stir in the parsley, lemon juice, shallot, ginger, and some pepper.

Preheat a grill to medium.

Add the shrimp to the grill and cook, turning as needed, until charred in places, curled, and pink throughout, about 5 minutes total. Transfer to a clean, shallow serving bowl or rimmed platter.

Pour the parsley oil mixture over the shrimp, tossing to coat. Sprinkle with chili flakes (if using) or more salt, if desired, and serve warm.

Sausage-Stuffed Fresh Cherry Peppers with Cheese and Bread Crumbs (page 162)

GRILLED LOBSTER TAILS

with fire-roasted tomatoes, corn, and butter

When they do serve lobster meat, Italians often do it still in the shell, sometimes grilled with oil and herbs, and other times stewed into a sauce with tomatoes and served with long pasta—though that is arguably more of an Italian-American preparation. Taking a little inspiration from both, I grill the tails and serve them with juicy tomatoes blackened lightly over the fire, and, of course, corn—without which no summer lobster dish would feel complete. It's delicious also with tomatillos, the tart, green cousins to the tomato, which you no longer will find in Italy but that are rumored to have been just as plentiful once as the red tomato there. Any way you serve it, it's a grand, generous dish.

6 [6 to 8 oz, or 170 to 230 g, each] fresh lobster tails

12 small yellow or red tomatoes [about 1 lb, or 455 g, total] on the vine, or medium tomatillos, husked and rinsed

4 to 6 large ears fresh corn, shucked and halved

2 small garlic heads, tops sliced off

Extra-virgin olive oil, for cooking and serving

Kosher salt

3 lemons, halved crosswise

1 bunch fresh dill (optional), for garnish

Freshly ground black pepper

Melted or clarified unsalted butter, for serving

SERVES 6 TO 12

Rinse or remove any innards from the lobster tails as needed. Using a large sharp knife or kitchen shears, halve the tails lengthwise, starting from the open (body) side and cutting through the meat and surrounding shells. Do not cut all the way through the last ½ in [12 mm] of meat or the flippers; leave this part intact. The tails should look like a "Y" shape when you're done.

Preheat a grill to high heat.

Rub the tails, tomatoes, corn, and garlic heads all over with olive oil and season with salt. Place on a baking sheet and set next to the grill.

Place the corn and garlic at the edges of the grill or wherever the temperature is slightly cooler. Put the lemons cut-side down in a hotter zone. Add the lobster tails to the hottest area of the grill in a single layer. Once the lemons are well charred on the cut sides, about 5 minutes, remove them.

Cook the lobster, turning as needed, until the shells are bright red and charred in places and the tail meat looks opaque, 6 to 8 minutes total. Cook the corn and garlic, turning or stacking the cobs occasionally to avoid over-blackening, until the kernels and garlic heads are charred and tender, about 15 minutes.

Transfer everything to the baking sheet and keep warm. Quickly add the tomatoes to the grill and cook, turning or shifting occasionally, until well charred and softened but not mushy or leaking, 3 to 4 minutes. Transfer to the baking sheet.

To serve, line a large platter with fresh dill sprigs (if using) and arrange the tails, corn, and garlic atop it. (If serving each guest half of a tail, cut the tails fully in half through the flippers.)

Drizzle the tomatoes with a little olive oil, and season with salt and pepper. Serve these on the side.

Season the melted butter generously with salt, and brush some of it on the lobster and corn. Serve everything hot with more butter or olive oil on the side for dipping.

My first time ever visiting Italy was in the early fall, when it seemed like everyone everywhere was out on the cobblestone streets, dining and drinking and trying to hold on to the last of the long, warm days. Coming from America, where even at a young age we seem to be constantly rushing from one engagement to the next, I was charmed at the silent commitment everyone shared during this season to making time to sit, talk, and eat. Fall is also the time that walking through Italian markets can feel like stepping into a storybook—the old wooden crates, rhythmic accents, and charming vendors make you want to stay all day. Some of them will practically force squash, tomatoes, and eggplant into your brown paper bag, not wanting you to miss their incredible flavor.

While we don't always have access to cobblestone markets, we can still indulge in the spirit of Italy in the fall by putting greater emphasis on generosity and slowness. It doesn't take much to be the one that kick-starts the planning of more gatherings. And that all starts with what to serve.

F A L L

POTATO SALAD WITH BLACK FIGS

and pancetta drippings vinaigrette

Potatoes are up there with tomatoes in terms of Italian vegetable loyalties. Italians classically serve them in simple ways, the cooked flesh smashed into breads or pasta, or roasted or boiled and then doused in olive oil and salt. But here, they're bathed in the drippings from crisping pancetta and tossed with one of the country's best fruits—fresh black figs. The fruits' honey-like insides work so well with the smoky, salty pancetta and a bright vinaigrette.

If you've missed the window for fresh figs—usually the late summer to early fall—you can use good-quality chopped dried figs. Any type of tiny potatoes will do, but reds and blues are so beautiful with the deep purple skins of the figs.

1½ lb [680 g] baby red and blue potatoes

1 tsp kosher salt, plus more as needed

1 Tbsp extra-virgin olive oil

2 tsp cider vinegar

2 tsp fresh lemon juice

1½ tsp Dijon mustard

1 tsp distilled white vinegar

Freshly ground black pepper

3 Tbsp finely diced pancetta

½ tsp black or brown mustard seeds

6 fresh, ripe black figs [4 oz, or 115 g, total], halved or quartered

Fresh thyme, marjoram, or chopped Italian parsley leaves, for serving

SERVES 6 TO 8

In a medium pot, combine the potatoes with enough water to cover by 1 in [2.5 cm]. Season the water with 1 tsp of salt and bring to a boil over high heat. Once boiling, cook until the potatoes feel fully tender when poked with a paring knife, but the skins are still intact, 15 to 18 minutes. Strain and let cool.

Meanwhile, make the dressing. In a medium bowl, whisk the olive oil, cider vinegar, lemon juice, mustard, white vinegar, and a pinch each of salt and pepper.

In a small skillet over medium-low heat, cook the pancetta, stirring occasionally, until most of the fat has rendered out and the pancetta is crispy and lightly browned in places, about 5 minutes. Transfer the pancetta to a small bowl and reserve the drippings in the pan.

Halve the potatoes with a sharp knife and place in a wide, shallow serving bowl. Drizzle with the dressing and toss gently and briefly to coat. Drizzle with the warm pancetta drippings. Garnish with the mustard seeds, figs, crispy pancetta, and some herb leaves. Serve immediately.

WARM OLIVES

with chorizo, sage, and orange

Warming olives before serving them is an easy trick that lends this ordinary, some might say overused, antipasto a new feel. But I like to go a step further and flavor the warmed olives, pairing them with juicy citrus wedges and crispy bits of seared, spicy sausage. Crisping rounds of dried chorizo in the pan allows their oils to flavor the olives, and also helps the flavors of the vinegar, mustard, garlic, and citrus zest adhere.

1 medium [about 4-oz, or 115-g] satsuma mandarin, clementine, or tangerine

¼ cup plus 1 Tbsp very thinly sliced dried chorizo [1¼ oz, or 35 g, total]

2 Tbsp extra-virgin olive oil

1 medium garlic clove, minced

1 star anise (optional)

½ tsp grainy mustard

½ tsp white wine vinegar or cider vinegar

2 cups [7 oz, or 200 g] mixed green pitted olives, (see Sidebar) drained of any liquids

5 small fresh sage leaves

SERVES 4 TO 6

Using a vegetable peeler, peel 3 large strips of zest off the mandarin and reserve. Peel the remainder of the skin and discard. Break the flesh into segments and reserve.

Set all your ingredients individually next to the stove. In a small pan over medium heat, combine the chorizo and 1 Tbsp of olive oil. Cook, tossing occasionally with tongs, until the chorizo is sizzling and lightly crispy, about 2 minutes. Add the remaining 1 Tbsp of oil, the garlic, star anise (if using), reserved zest, mustard, and vinegar. Stir well.

Add the olives and cook, stirring until warm, about 2 minutes. Pour the mixture into a serving bowl.

Turn the heat to medium-low and add the mandarin slices. Cook for 30 seconds and transfer to the bowl. Stir. Add the sage leaves to the hot skillet and cook, turning, until lightly seared, 1 minute. Transfer to the bowl. Serve warm.

Choosing the Right Olive

Feel free to tinker with the mix of olives, but firm green olives—such as Castelvetrano or Cerignola—stand up to cooking quite well and give the dish amazing color. For this preparation, I like to buy mine already pitted from the olive bar.

OLIVE OIL–MARINATED GOAT CHEESE

with celery and mountain herbs

This easy, elegant antipasto is inspired by a preparation in northeastern Italy's Valle d'Aosta: soft, salty rounds of cheese smothered in a mixture of marinated celery, wintry herbs, and lots of good olive oil. Delicious from the start, the dish gets more succulent as time goes by, the oil softening and flavoring the cheese.

When shopping, give the goat cheese logs a little squeeze and choose a brand that's on the firmer side. And remember to slice the celery very thinly, almost to the point of translucence.

One 6-oz [170-g] log goat cheese (chèvre)

2 celery stalks [about 4 oz, or 115 g, total], halved lengthwise and very thinly sliced

1 tsp very finely chopped fresh sage

1 tsp very finely chopped fresh thyme leaves

½ tsp very finely chopped fresh rosemary leaves

⅛ packed tsp finely grated lemon zest

2 tsp white wine vinegar

¼ tsp finely grated fresh garlic

⅛ tsp fine sea salt or kosher salt

1 generous pinch of ground nutmeg

5 Tbsp [75 ml] extra-virgin olive oil

Freshly ground black pepper

Crusty bread, warmed if desired, for serving

SERVES 6 TO 8

Carefully slice the goat cheese logs into ¼-in- [6-mm-] thick rounds. (If the cheese crumbles when sliced, use unflavored dental floss to help cut the rounds; see Sidebar.)

In a medium-rimmed plate or flat-bottomed shallow bowl, carefully place the cheese rounds in a single layer, leaving a little room between each. (If they are not perfect shapes, don't worry; they'll be covered in oil and toppings soon.) Set aside at room temperature.

In a separate medium bowl, combine the celery, herbs, lemon zest, vinegar, garlic, salt, nutmeg, and 1 Tbsp of olive oil. Stir well. Spoon the mixture over and around the cheese rounds. Drizzle with the remaining 4 Tbsp [60 ml] of olive oil. Sprinkle generously with pepper. If you can, let the cheese marinate at room temperature for 30 minutes, or up to 1 hour. Serve with forks and crusty bread for scooping up bites of the cheese and toppings.

Slicing Goat Cheese

To help cut particularly crumbly goat cheeses into stable slices, try using unflavored dental floss, pulling the floss down through the cheese log to create even rounds. Once on the serving plate, tidy up the slices as needed, pressing them back together into compact circles. Cover any imperfections later with the celery topping.

ROASTED ESCAROLE

with pistachios, labneh, and cayenne

Escarole comes to the market late in the year. Growing up, we ate it weekly in the fall and winter, stewed with softened garlic and cannellini beans in a thin broth. I've taken to roasting it in the oven, where the leaves' centers retain a little crunch and their edges soften, moisten, and crisp lightly. Rubbing them with chopped garlic and good olive oil before roasting gives the bitter greens some sweetness and spice. And if you can't find labneh, which is like a thicker version of Greek yogurt, use whole-milk Greek yogurt.

One 7-oz [200-g] head escarole,
leaves washed well, dried, and coarsely torn

3 Tbsp extra-virgin olive oil

2½ tsp finely chopped fresh garlic

Scant ¼ tsp kosher salt

Freshly ground black pepper

Ground cayenne pepper

¼ cup [60 g] labneh or plain,
full-fat Greek yogurt

½ lemon, for squeezing

¼ cup [35 g] unsalted raw or
roasted pistachios, coarsely chopped

SERVES 4 TO 6

Preheat the oven to 375°F [190°C] and set a rack in the top third of the oven.

Transfer the escarole to a large baking sheet. Drizzle the leaves with the olive oil, sprinkle with the chopped garlic and salt, and season generously with pepper. Toss, rubbing the leaves with the oil to coat. Spread them again on the sheet in an even layer with any curly sides facing up.

Transfer the sheet to the top rack of the oven and roast until the leaves are just wilted and some of the ends have browned slightly, 7 to 9 minutes. Remove and sprinkle very lightly with cayenne.

Serve from the baking sheet, or transfer to a large serving platter, spreading the leaves across the platter. Dollop the labneh in small piles all around the escarole. Squeeze with lemon juice and sprinkle with the pistachios. Serve warm.

Who Needs a Platter?

You can garnish and serve this dish right atop the baking sheet you cooked it on. The residual heat will keep it warmer longer and lightly melt the labneh.

SEARED MUSHROOMS

with dried currants, purple radishes, and kale

The key to the best-tasting mushrooms is to cook them in a scorching-hot pan with plenty of oil, while not adding too many to the pan at once. The latter tip helps them sear deeply instead of steam. Here I cook sliced mushrooms in batches, then mix them with some fluffy kale and a little dried fruit—a very Italian addition—that helps balance the mushrooms' pungent savory flavors. You can substitute finely chopped prunes or raisins for the dried currants if they are tricky to find.

6 Tbsp [90 ml] extra-virgin olive oil

12 oz [340 g] maitake, cremini, or small porcini mushrooms, cut into bite-size portions (if using cremini or porcini, thinly slice)

Kosher salt

Freshly ground black pepper

2 packed cups [70 g] finely chopped Tuscan (dino or lacinato) kale

2 tsp minced fresh garlic

2 Tbsp dried currants

1 medium purple radish [3 oz, or 85 g], peeled, quartered lengthwise, and thinly sliced [½ cup], or ½ cup thinly sliced red radishes

1 Tbsp fresh lemon juice, or more as desired

SERVES 4

In a large skillet over high heat, heat 3 Tbsp of olive oil. Once hot, add half of the mushrooms (they should sizzle significantly when they hit the oil). Season generously with salt and pepper. Cook, stirring sparingly, until well seared, 3 to 4 minutes. Transfer the mushrooms to a large serving bowl or platter, then quickly add 2 Tbsp more olive oil and the remaining half of the mushrooms to the pan; repeat the cooking process. Transfer to the bowl or platter.

Lower the heat to medium and quickly add the remaining 1 Tbsp of olive oil, the kale, and the garlic. Season with salt and stir to distribute. Add 2 Tbsp of water and cook, stirring constantly, until the kale is slightly tenderized and the water has evaporated, 30 seconds to 1 minute. Transfer to the serving vessel with the mushrooms and toss gently.

Sprinkle with the dried currants and scatter the radishes on top. Drizzle with the lemon juice and sprinkle with more salt and pepper. Toss well to combine. Taste and adjust the seasoning as needed, and serve.

SEARED SHRIMP

with braised savoy cabbage

This unassuming dish is one of my favorites to serve and prepare. I first tried cabbage in a similar style at a Sardinian restaurant, where they boiled the leaves in salted water, then seasoned them aggressively with olive oil. This quick-braised version is more flavorful and saves boiling time, and with the shrimp on top, becomes something surprising.

I love Savoy cabbage, a delicate, webbed variety that is milder, sweeter, and more tender than green cabbage, which you can find in the fall. If not, napa cabbage is a fair substitute.

5 Tbsp [75 ml] extra-virgin olive oil
plus more for drizzling

½ medium white onion [3½ oz, or 100 g],
very thinly sliced

Kosher salt

5 large garlic cloves, finely chopped

6 packed cups [12 oz, or 340 g] thinly sliced
Savoy cabbage, from about 1 medium cabbage

1 Tbsp white wine vinegar or distilled white vinegar

¼ tsp sugar

Freshly ground black pepper

1½ lb [680 g] shrimp, about 32 extra-large or
18 jumbo, shelled except for their tails and deveined

SERVES 8

Preheat the broiler to its highest setting and set a rack in the top third of the oven.

Meanwhile, in a large pot or Dutch oven over medium heat, heat 3 Tbsp of the olive oil. Once hot, add the onion and about ⅛ tsp of salt. Cook, stirring occasionally, until softened slightly, about 2 minutes. Add the garlic. Cook, stirring constantly, for 2 minutes more (the amount of raw garlic may seem like a lot while you're adding it, but, believe me, it is the perfect amount). Add the cabbage, ⅓ cup [80 ml] of water, the vinegar, ¼ tsp more salt, the sugar, and ⅛ tsp of pepper. Cook, stirring occasionally, until the cabbage is softened, 10 to 12 minutes.

Place the shrimp on a rimmed baking sheet. Sprinkle with ⅛ tsp each of salt and pepper and the remaining 2 Tbsp of olive oil. Toss briefly and spread in a single layer. Broil until the shrimp are lightly seared, opaque, and curled, 6 to 8 minutes. Remove.

Taste the cabbage and adjust the seasoning, if needed. Using tongs, spread the cabbage on a large serving plate. Top with the shrimp and drizzle lightly with more olive oil or sprinkle with more salt and pepper. Serve warm.

CLAMS WITH BROCCOLI RABE

and crispy prosciutto in tomato-wine sauce

I am a broccoli rabe, or *rapini*, junkie—a lover of its assertive bitterness. So, this dish came from my desire to combine two of my favorite foods: broccoli rabe and fresh, juicy clams. Serving only the broccoli rabe florets and little of their fibrous stems, and nestling the pieces in a little tomato sauce, white wine, and the salty brine from the clams tames some of the vegetable's pungency. The dish takes about 15 minutes start to finish, and it's one of my favorites to serve straight out of the skillet, on the coffee table, with a bottle of good wine.

¼ cup [61 g] canned tomato purée

2 Tbsp dry white wine

1 Tbsp finely chopped fresh garlic

¼ cup [60 ml] extra-virgin olive oil

4 thin slices [about 1 oz, or 30 g] prosciutto

¼ medium yellow onion, chopped
[¼ packed cup, or 35 g]

2 lb [910 g] littleneck clams or similar small clams, such as Manila, purged (see Sidebar, page 103)

3 packed cups [about 3¾ oz, or 105 g] broccoli rabe, a mix of florets and leaves (no thick stems)

Freshly ground black pepper

Chili flakes, for serving

Crusty bread, for serving

SERVES 4

Set a paper towel–lined plate next to the stove. In a medium bowl, stir together the tomato purée, wine, and garlic and set this next to the stove.

In a large skillet with a lid over medium-high heat, heat the olive oil. Once hot, add the prosciutto and cook, turning occasionally with tongs, until lightly browned on both sides, 4 to 5 minutes. Quickly transfer the prosciutto slices to the prepared plate and lower the heat to medium.

Add the onion to the skillet and cook, stirring constantly, for 30 seconds. Stir in the tomato mixture, then stir in the clams. Cover the pan and cook, shaking the pan occasionally, until the clams open, 5 to 6 minutes. Add the broccoli rabe and a generous amount of black pepper. Stir to help nestle the broccoli pieces into the sauce. Cover the pan again and cook until the broccoli rabe florets are firm-tender and bright green, 3 to 4 minutes. Remove the lid and discard any clams that did not open.

Serve warm with chili flakes and crusty bread.

SLICED PORK SAUSAGE

with seared cauliflower and fennel

The Italian culinary repertoire is fat with pork dishes, especially in northern Italy where there are more kinds of pork sausage than one can count. When making this as one of many plates for a party, I cut the rich meat with plenty of vegetables to prevent the dish from being too filling—in this case, some thin slices of cauliflower and cool, crisp pieces of fennel—an ingredient I love with pork. You can cook the sausages slightly in advance and keep them warm in aluminum foil, but do not slice them until just before serving.

VEGETABLES AND SAUSAGE

Kosher salt

1 medium [7-oz, or 200-g] fennel bulb, trimmed, halved lengthwise, and thinly sliced, fronds reserved

4 Tbsp [60 ml] plus 1 tsp extra-virgin olive oil

1 medium [about 1¼-lb, or 570-g] head cauliflower or romanesco, trimmed, florets and stems thinly sliced

6 links mild herbed pork sausage [about 2 lb, or 910 g], pierced in a few places with a paring knife

DRESSING

5 Tbsp [75 ml] fresh lemon juice

2 Tbsp extra-virgin olive oil

2 tsp cider vinegar

½ tsp honey

Kosher salt

Freshly ground black pepper

½ tsp yellow mustard seeds (optional)

Chili powder, for serving (optional)

SERVES 6 TO 8

PREPARE THE VEGETABLES: Fill a large bowl with cool water and add a generous pinch of salt. Whisk to incorporate. Add the fennel slices and set the bowl aside.

In a large skillet over medium-high heat, heat 2 Tbsp of olive oil. Once hot, add half the cauliflower pieces and spread them into a single layer. Sprinkle generously with salt and cook, gently turning once, until browned slightly on both sides, 6 to 7 minutes total. Transfer to a plate. Return the skillet to the heat and add 2 Tbsp more olive oil. Season with salt and repeat the cooking process with the remaining cauliflower pieces. Transfer to the plate when done.

COOK THE SAUSAGES: Add the sausages and the remaining 1 tsp of olive oil to the skillet and lower the heat to medium. Cook until deeply browned on one side, 12 to 14 minutes. Turn and cook until well browned on the remaining side and cooked throughout, 12 to 14 minutes more. Remove the sausages to a cutting board and let cool slightly.

MEANWHILE, MAKE THE DRESSING: In a medium bowl, whisk the lemon juice, olive oil, vinegar, honey, and a pinch each of salt and pepper until well combined.

Slice the sausages on a long diagonal into ½-in- [12-mm-] thick pieces.

continued

Arrange the sausage on a large serving platter. Carefully nestle the cauliflower slices among the sausage pieces, overlapping the two slightly. Drain the fennel well and pat dry. Sprinkle the pieces in between and around the platter. Drizzle with the dressing. Garnish with the mustard seeds, fennel fronds, and a light dusting of black pepper and chili powder, if desired, and serve.

BRAISED PORK

with garlic, bay leaves, and orange peel

Brasato is a preparation of slow-braised meat, usually a large cut of beef or pork, cooked in a sealed pot with seasonings. This version is not like traditional *brasato* in that I chose to cut the meat, in this case pork shoulder, into smaller pieces so more of it comes in contact with the juices and rendered fat in the bottom of the roasting pan. Leave the majority of fat on the pieces while they cook: the fat renders out and the meat ends up slowly simmering inside it. You can remove any large pieces of fat later, while the meat crisps up in a skillet after roasting.

4 lb [1.8 kg] boneless pork shoulder, meat and fat cut into 1½-in [4-cm] cubes

½ medium yellow onion, chopped

5 garlic cloves, peeled

4 bay leaves

3 large strips orange peel (no pith)

1 Tbsp extra-virgin olive oil or lard

1 Tbsp kosher salt

½ tsp dried thyme

Freshly ground black pepper

Crusty bread, for serving

Lemon wedges, for squeezing (optional)

SERVES 10

Preheat the oven to 425°F [220°C].

In a large Dutch oven or roasting pan, combine the pork pieces, onion, garlic, bay leaves, orange peel, olive oil, salt, thyme, and a generous pinch of pepper. Toss with your hands or stir briefly to incorporate the seasonings evenly. Spread the ingredients evenly in the pan.

Cover the pot or tightly seal the roasting pan with aluminum foil. Bake until the pork is tender and juicy, 2 hours. Carefully remove the pot from the oven (be careful when opening it, as it will release very hot steam). At this point you can shred and serve the pork without searing, refrigerate overnight for reheating the next day, or sear and serve the pork immediately.

When ready to serve, set a large skillet over medium-high heat and drizzle with some of the rendered fat from the pan. Once the skillet is hot, add half the pork (get rid of any large chunks of fat as desired) and break up the meat pieces slightly using tongs or two forks, if desired. Cook, undisturbed, until the meat is seared on one side, about 2 minutes. Stir and cook for another 1 to 2 minutes on the other side. Transfer to a serving bowl and repeat with the remaining pork.

Taste and adjust the seasonings as needed. Serve the pork warm, drizzled with pan drippings and squeezed with lemon, if desired, with crusty bread.

MORTADELLA AND FONTINA SLAB PIE

with caramelized fennel

This flaky, comforting puff pastry is reminiscent of a ham and cheese croissant, but without the labor of from-scratch pastry, and with tender, braised fennel. It also, importantly, features mortadella, the supreme charcuterie of Bologna, a delightfully floppy pink salumi with visible, delicate morsels of pork fat. You can find mortadella at many grocery stores and certainly Italian markets. The best versions contain little flecks of green pistachio.

1 Tbsp unsalted butter

1 medium [7-oz, or 200-g] fennel bulb, thinly sliced into ½-in- [12-mm-] long pieces

Kosher salt

Freshly ground black pepper

2 tsp Dijon mustard, plus more for serving

1 large egg

All-purpose flour, for dusting

1 [7-oz, or 200-g] sheet frozen puff pastry, thawed in the refrigerator for 2 to 3 hours

8 oz [230 g] very thinly sliced mortadella with pistachios

4 oz [115 g] shredded fontina cheese

SERVES 8

Bigger is better.

Making one large pastry is easier and faster than assembling a bunch of smaller, handheld pastries. Cut this larger pie into as many pieces as makes sense for your guest list.

In a large skillet over medium heat, melt the butter. Add the fennel and season lightly with salt and pepper. Cook, stirring frequently, until softened slightly, 5 to 6 minutes. Stir in the mustard and turn off the heat. Let cool slightly.

Meanwhile, preheat the oven to 400°F [200°C] and set a rimless metal baking sheet on the center rack of the oven or overturn a rimmed metal baking sheet (make sure it's level).

In a small bowl, beat the egg with 1 tsp of water. Set aside.

Line a large flat cutting board with a piece of parchment paper. On a lightly floured work surface, roll out the puff pastry to a thin sheet about 14 by 15 in [35.5 by 38 cm] in size. Carefully transfer the pastry dough to the parchment-lined board. Starting at one of the shorter sides, top half the pastry dough evenly with the mortadella slices, leaving a 1 in [2.5 cm] border around the edges. Add half of the cheese, the fennel mixture, and the remaining cheese. Brush the edges of the dough nearest the filling with the egg wash. Carefully fold the other half of the dough over the fillings, stretching lightly as needed to cover. Crimp the edges with a fork to seal.

Brush the entire top and edges of the dough with the egg wash. Sprinkle the dough lightly with salt and pepper. Score the top surface of the pie a few times with a paring knife to help steam escape while baking.

continued

Carefully slide the pie and the parchment paper onto the preheated baking sheet in the oven. Bake until golden brown on top, bubbling on the inside, and the bottom is solid and slightly browned, 25 to 30 minutes.

Remove and let cool for 5 to 10 minutes. Serve warm, cut into squares and with more Dijon mustard on the side.

ROASTED BROCCOLI AND GARLIC STROMBOLI

with mozzarella

When we were in grade school, my best friend's parents owned a pizza restaurant. We grew up zipping around the pizza kitchen, weaving between the legs of the *pizzaioli* who, looking back, I'm sure were furious. Even more delicious than their pizzas were their stuffed breads, like a broccoli and mozzarella–filled stromboli. Garlicky and lightly crisp with layers of warm cheese and bite-size cubes of caramelized broccoli, this one wins over everyone.

Do your best to stretch the dough as thinly as possible without breaking it, as this prevents a too-thick crust. If that's not your forte, try my trick using the edges of a baking sheet to help.

One 1-lb [455-g] ball good-quality pizza dough, fully risen and at room temperature

All-purpose flour, as needed

About 1 lb [455 g] broccoli with stems, about 2 full heads

2 Tbsp extra-virgin olive oil, plus more for brushing

½ tsp kosher salt

Freshly ground black pepper

1 Tbsp plus 1 tsp finely chopped garlic

2¼ cups [6⅓ oz, or 180 g] shredded mozzarella (not fresh)

SERVES 4 TO 8

Be sure the pizza dough is lightly floured and at room temperature before beginning.

Using a sharp knife, trim the woody bottoms, usually 1½ to 2 in [4 to 5 cm], off the broccoli stems. Using a sharp knife or vegetable peeler, slice away the outer peel from the remaining stems and discard the peel. Dice the remaining stems into ½-in [12-mm] pieces. Tear or cut the florets into ½-in [12-mm] pieces, too. You should have about 4 slightly heaping cups of broccoli total.

In a large nonstick skillet over medium-high heat, heat the olive oil. Add the broccoli, salt, and a generous pinch of pepper. Cook, stirring frequently, until firm-tender, 6 to 7 minutes. Add the garlic and cook for 1 minute more. Remove and let cool almost completely.

Preheat the oven to 425°F [220°C].

Overturn a 13-by-17-in [33-by-43-cm] baking sheet facedown on a clean counter with one of the long sides facing you. Begin stretching the pizza dough: Pick it up slightly off the counter and, turning the dough like a steering wheel, use the outside of your closed fist and your fingertips around the perimeter to stretch it—never stretch the middle, as it can cause breakage. When the dough starts to become a lot larger and thinner, drape one side of the dough over the long side of the

continued

baking sheet farthest from you, tucking the dough slightly under the sheet to help secure it. (The baking sheet is a cheat that's just here to help you stretch the dough and keep it from retracting while you fill the stromboli.) The remaining dough should be hanging toward you, longer than the baking sheet and maybe even slightly hanging off the counter so gravity can help continue to stretch it.

Starting about 4 in [10 cm] away from the dough's edge that lines the farthest edge of the baking sheet, begin scattering ¾ cup [60 g] of the shredded cheese in a line across the baking sheet's long side (the line of cheese should be about 3 in, or 7.5 cm, wide). Leave about ½ in [12 mm] of dough free on either short end of the line. To the cheese pile, add ¾ cup (one-third of the total) of the cooled broccoli, spreading it evenly down the line. Wrap the reserved 4-in [10-cm] edge over the filling, pulling it gently to fully cover the ingredients. Repeat this two more times, starting the next line of filling right next to the existing pile, then rolling the existing mound of ingredients on top as if you were rolling a scroll. Once the third layer of filling is covered by the other two layers of filling and dough, wrap the final and remaining piece of clean dough fully around the mounded ingredients at least once, or ideally twice if you have the

dough to spare. Pull, press, and stretch the stromboli slightly so the seams are facing downward, the filling looks evenly distributed, and the top is relatively flat.

Turn the baking sheet right-side up and position the stromboli inside, turning the dough diagonally on the baking sheet if needed to fit. Using a paring knife, cut just a few small slits in the top of the stromboli to help steam escape while baking. Brush the top and sides all over with olive oil and bake until the outsides are well browned, but not burning on the bottom, and the cheese is fully melted, 35 to 40 minutes. Remove and let cool for at least 10 to 15 minutes. Using a serrated knife, slice into 2-in [5-cm-] thick slices and serve warm.

"SIX-FOOT SUB" BAGUETTES

When I was growing up, no backyard family gathering was complete without a monstrous, literally six-foot-long, sub from the Italian bakery. I'm still nostalgic for them. So, now I make my own using a toasted, open-face baguette and a homemade olive salad, which I season with an easy balsamic vinaigrette. Using a good-quality aged balsamic vinegar makes a significant difference in the flavor.

1 baguette, halved crosswise sandwich style

1 cup [126 g] mixed green and red pitted olives, such as Castelvetrano and Kalamata, coarsely chopped

1 tsp balsamic vinegar

1 Tbsp extra-virgin olive oil

1 Tbsp finely chopped red onion

2 tsp finely chopped fresh Italian parsley leaves

¾ lb [340 g] mixed Italian salumi, such as soppressata, hot coppa, prosciutto, and bresaola, sliced as thinly as possible

4 oz [115 g] thinly sliced, narrow pieces of provolone cheese (about 16 small slices)

SERVES 12

Preheat the oven to 350°F [180°C].

Place the baguette halves in the oven and bake until lightly toasted and warmed, 5 to 7 minutes.

Meanwhile, in a medium bowl, combine the olives, vinegar, olive oil, red onion, and parsley. Stir well.

Retrieve the baguette pieces and lay them cut-side up on a counter or board. Begin to layer the salumi and cheese onto the bread, scrunching up the salumi pieces as you go, then following with a slice of cheese. Repeat until both bread pieces are covered. Spoon some of the olive mixture and its juices into the crevices of some of the salumi pieces.

Using a large sharp knife, cut the open-faced sandwich into whatever size pieces you desire (avoid a "sawing" motion and instead press down hard to cut straight through). Serve.

TRI-COLOR BEETS

with garlic and lemon aioli

Aioli is a rich, strongly flavored emulsion of garlic paste and olive oil, used on Italy's Ligurian coast near the border of France. I adore beets—especially the yellow and pink ones, which I boil here for ease (and because roasting can take an eternity)—but, let's face it, they are basically a vehicle for eating aioli.

Whipping up aioli from scratch can be a chore, and I honestly think this version, made using store-bought mayonnaise, might be better anyway. I am a loyalist to Hellman's brand (judge me if you will), which is what I use here. But to each their own. Start by adding a little less olive oil if you're using a smoother, runnier brand.

BEETS

1½ lb [680 g] beets, about 7 medium,
a mix of yellow, red, and Chioggia

Kosher salt

1 Tbsp extra-virgin olive oil

AIOLI

6 Tbsp [90 g] mayonnaise

1 Tbsp plus 1 tsp extra-virgin olive oil

1 Tbsp fresh lemon juice

½ tsp finely grated garlic, grated on a Microplane

Scant ½ tsp finely grated lemon zest

Pinch of kosher salt

Generous pinch of freshly ground black pepper

SERVES 6 TO 8

COOK THE BEETS: Add the beets to a medium pot, then add enough water to cover by at least 1 in [2.5 cm]. Season the pot generously with salt and bring to a low boil over high heat. Cook until the beets feel completely tender when poked through the center with a paring knife, 45 minutes to 1 hour. Drain and let cool slightly.

Using the pads of your fingers, or paper towels if needed, and holding the beets under cool running water, rub away the skins and discard. Peel away any stubborn skins with a vegetable peeler, if needed. Halve or quarter the beets through the stem side, and transfer to a bowl. Drizzle with the olive oil and sprinkle with salt.

MAKE THE AIOLI: In a medium bowl, combine the mayonnaise, olive oil, lemon juice, garlic, lemon zest, and a pinch each of salt and pepper. Stir well. Taste and adjust the seasoning as needed.

Spread a little of the aioli in the bottom of a serving plate or serving bowl. Add the beets. Serve with the remaining aioli.

MINI "PORCHETTA"

with radish giardiniera and pork fat toasts

A specialty of central Italy, *porchetta* traditionally meant a boned piglet, often flavored with wild fennel from the region, roasted on a spit, and served with thick chunks of rustic bread. Over time, we have come to know the dish as its oven-friendly variation, typically made from a skin-on pork belly wrapped around a boneless loin and tied. It's magnificent, but an undertaking, and a little too much meat for the antipasti course.

I've minimized the work by concentrating on the skin and belly—the best parts anyway—and seasoning them with what's come to be the classic seasonings: plenty of fennel seed and rosemary. The resulting niblets of crispy-skinned pork are served atop toasts brushed with pork fat.

Radish Giardiniera (page 28) or Classic Giardiniera (page 27), for serving

One 1½-lb [680-g] piece skin-on pork belly with a generous proportion of meat to fat (see Sidebar)

1½ tsp kosher salt, plus more as needed

½ tsp sugar

¼ tsp coarsely ground black pepper

1 Tbsp finely chopped fresh Italian parsley or sage leaves, or a mix

½ tsp coarsely chopped fresh or dried rosemary leaves

1 tsp fennel seeds

8 garlic cloves, peeled

1 loaf ciabatta, halved crosswise down the center

SERVES 8

The ideal pork belly piece for this dish is on the thicker side and has a substantial amount of pink meat in proportion to the fat. If needed, you can cook the pork in advance and reheat in a low oven before serving.

Make sure your giardiniera is prepared and cooling or chilled before you begin.

Preheat the oven to 325°F [165°C] and set a rack in the top third of the oven.

Using a very sharp knife, cut the pork belly into slabs 2½ to 3 in [5 to 7.5 cm] wide. (This will probably mean 2 long strips; the length doesn't matter that much, so if you need to trim them further to fit into your roasting vessel, that's fine.) Working crosswise across each slab, score the top of the skin about every ⅓ in [8 mm], cutting through some of the top layer of fat as well, but do not cut through the meat. Pat the meat and skin dry with paper towels and transfer to a rimmed baking sheet or glass baking dish.

Season the meat and skin all over with the 1½ tsp of salt, the sugar, and pepper, rubbing to adhere. Distribute the herbs and fennel seeds all over the meat and skin and rub to adhere. Position the meat pieces skin-side up on the baking sheet at least 1 in [2.5 cm] apart.

continued

Transfer to the oven and roast for 2 hours. Raise the heat to 425°F [220°C] and add the garlic to the pan. Continue roasting until the pork skin is well browned and blistered, 10 to 20 minutes more.

Remove and tent the pork with aluminum foil. Do not turn off the oven. Add the bread halves to the oven and bake until lightly toasted, about 8 minutes.

Meanwhile, thinly slice the pork into pieces where the knife scores lie.

Remove the bread and lightly brush the insides with the drippings from the baking pan. If desired, you can slather the bread with the cooked garlic cloves, or serve them on the side. Cut the bread into rough squares [about 3 in, or 7.5 cm, each].

Serve the bread either alongside the pork and giardiniera and have people assemble their own bites, or build small open-face sandwiches with the bread and pork, topping with some of the giardiniera.

BREADED CHICKEN CUTLETS

with garlic-roasted cranberries

These crispy chicken cutlets were a weeknight staple when I was growing up. My mom took care to pound them thin, so the white meat cooked through just in the time it took to turn them deeply golden brown on both sides. We ate them with ketchup to moisten each bite (certainly not Italian, but delicious), so I'm sure my family will laugh that I've fancied them up here: in place of ketchup are tart and sweet fresh cranberries, roasted with honey, herbs, and garlic. In the warmer seasons, you can use the same ingredients and preparation using tiny cherry tomatoes.

CRANBERRIES

3 cups [about 11 oz, or 310 g]
fresh cranberries or frozen, thawed

6 garlic cloves, in their skins

3 Tbsp extra-virgin olive oil

1 tsp honey

⅛ tsp kosher salt

Freshly ground black pepper

2 sprigs fresh thyme

1 sprig fresh rosemary, coarsely torn

2 fresh sage leaves

CHICKEN

3 boneless skinless chicken breasts
[1¼ lb, or 570 g, total]

2 large eggs

1½ tsp kosher salt, plus more as needed

¾ cup [105 g] dried bread crumbs

¾ tsp dried basil

¾ tsp dried parsley

½ tsp dried rosemary

½ cup [120 ml] extra-virgin olive oil,
plus more as needed for frying

SERVES 6 TO 8

Preheat the oven to 425°F [220°C].

MAKE THE CRANBERRIES: Line a baking sheet with parchment paper or foil and place the cranberries and garlic cloves on it. In a small saucepan over medium heat, heat the olive oil and honey until runny. Stir well and pour over the cranberries and garlic. Sprinkle with the salt and some pepper and stir well. Add the herb sprigs and leaves and roast until the cranberries are slightly charred and well shriveled, about 30 minutes.

MEANWHILE, MAKE THE CHICKEN: Using a long sharp knife, butterfly the chicken breasts crosswise, then cut each in half. One at a time, place each resulting piece between two large sheets of plastic wrap and, using a meat mallet or something sturdy like the bottom of a glass liquid measuring cup, pound the chicken ⅛ in [4 mm] thick (see Sidebar, page 127, for tips). Remove the pounded pieces from the plastic wrap and slice in half lengthwise again. (It's no big deal if the chicken shapes are different or uneven.)

continued

In a medium shallow bowl, beat the eggs with a pinch of salt. In a second medium shallow bowl or rimmed plate, mix the bread crumbs, dried herbs, and a generous pinch of salt. Season the chicken pieces all over with 1½ tsp of salt.

One by one, dip the chicken pieces in the egg mixture to coat. Let the excess drip back into the bowl, then dip the chicken into the bread crumb mixture, tossing and patting the cutlets so the bread crumbs adhere all over. Set on a large plate or baking sheet next to the stove. Line a plate with a few pieces of paper towel and place that nearby as well.

When all the chicken pieces are breaded, in a large nonstick skillet over medium-high heat, heat the olive oil until shimmering. Add a few cutlets in a single layer (the oil should sizzle significantly), allowing at least ½ in [12 mm] between pieces. Cook, turning once, until deeply golden brown and crispy on both sides, about 8 minutes total.

Transfer the cutlets to the paper towel–lined plate as they are done. Continue to add more breaded chicken to the pan where there's room. At the very last batch, you may need to add 1 to 2 Tbsp more olive oil. If you stack chicken pieces atop one another after frying, place a layer or two of paper towels in between the stacks.

Retrieve the cranberries. On a large serving platter, spread out the chicken pieces, overlapping slightly. Spoon some of the roasted cranberries, herb sprigs, and garlic on top and between the layers. Serve warm.

FRIED BEEF MEATBALLS

For generations in my family, meatballs were Sunday morning breakfast. My great-grandmother would fry them in olive oil, then place them on a roll, letting the oil drip right onto the bread to become the sandwich's only condiment. I use all beef because it's easy and what I grew up eating in our American kitchen, but you could split these into equal parts beef and veal if you'd like. The little specks of grease and the meaty perfume they kick off when frying are unavoidable, but use a splatter screen if you have one. These are best when hot, but still delicious at room temperature.

1 lb [455 g] well-raised ground beef

1 large egg

1 Tbsp plus 1 tsp finely grated, good-quality Pecorino Romano cheese

1 Tbsp dried bread crumbs

¼ tsp kosher salt

Freshly ground black pepper

1 Tbsp plus 2 tsp chopped fresh Italian parsley leaves

1 Tbsp finely chopped fresh basil leaves

2 tsp finely chopped garlic

½ cup [120 ml] olive oil, for frying

Italian bread or hard rolls, for serving (optional)

MAKES 8

In a large bowl, combine all of the ingredients except the olive oil and bread (if using). Drizzle the meatball mixture with 3 Tbsp of cool water. Using your fingers, stir everything well, breaking the egg as you go, until the ingredients are just combined. Do not overmix.

Form the meatball mixture into about 8 balls, ¼ cup or 2 oz [55 g] each in size. Flatten each slightly. Place them near the stove.

Set a large clean plate next to the stove and line it with a few layers of paper towels. In a large nonstick skillet over medium-high heat, heat the olive oil. Once hot, add the meatballs (the oil should sizzle when you add the meat), flattening the tops slightly with the back of a fork. Cook until deeply browned on one side, lowering the heat slightly or covering the pan with a splatter screen as needed, about 6 minutes. Using a fork, carefully turn the meatballs in the pan. Cook until deeply browned on the remaining side and fully cooked through, about 6 minutes more.

Transfer to the paper towel–lined plate and let cool ever so slightly. Serve immediately, with forks or for eating with fingers, with or without bread.

GRAZIE

It's no exaggeration to say I have been storing up ideas for this book for years. And in that course of time, so many people—knowingly or unknowingly—helped me turn it into a reality. First and foremost, my amazing husband who believes in me always, even when it means balancing book writing on the side of a full-time job and recipe testing on weeknights when I come home. Thank you for being my taste tester and sounding board, and partner in everything. Nothing I've ever achieved holds a candle to the bliss I feel having found you to share my life with.

I want to sincerely thank my mom, for relentlessly cooking at home while we were growing up and sparking a love in all of us for doing so, too. And Dad, I am so grateful that you both fearlessly introduced us to the great foods of the world while teaching us the importance of carrying on our family traditions. Thank you both for keeping us close with our grandparents and letting me be the first in our family to write down some of their recipes. And to my siblings, siblings-in-law, and my husband's and my entire immediate and extended families, who support us always, you are without a doubt the most important thing in our lives— and our favorite people to feed.

Thank you to Sarah Billingsley at Chronicle Books, who instantly understood, shared, and enhanced my vision for this book. To my editor, Camaren Subhiyah, it feels like kismet that you came to Chronicle right in time to partner with me on this project. Thank you for your intelligent edits and wise suggestions throughout the entire process.

A heartfelt thank you to Linda Pugliese, my fellow Italophile, for your stunning images and for rolling up your sleeves with me on every step of this shoot. To Vanessa Dina for your vision, enthusiasm, and unparalleled creativity, and to Paige Hicks and your team, for your genius way with props. I so appreciated and cherished my time bringing this book to life with you.

Thank you to our all-lady kitchen crew: Sadie Gelb and Liz Bossin, you were both sent by an angel and I could not have made it through the food styling without you. Each of you is full of so much talent and I'm thrilled to continue to watch you share it with the world.

Huge thanks to my recipe testers, including friends and family who stayed up late making dishes from this book and giving feedback on the recipes. Especially my friend Vic, who not only tested more dishes than anyone but also inspired a few. (You, too, Vinny, Dom, and Kathy.) And Jen, who lent more than a little moral support.

Finally, to my grandparents, who are no longer alive to read this note but I know can "hear" me wherever they are. You were and still are my everything—the reason I became a cook and found my love for Italy and our heritage, and the people I most aspire to be like. I miss the days of gathering with you and all of us, my favorite times around the table. Though no one's food will ever taste as good as yours, I hope this book makes you proud.

Grazie mille, from the bottom of my heart.

INDEX

STACY ADIMANDO is a food and travel writer, James Beard Award–winning cookbook author, and the executive editor at *Saveur* magazine. Her food and travel writing and recipes have been published by NPR, *Bon Appétit, Food & Wine, Condé Nast Traveler, Vogue, Forbes,* and many more.

Chronicle Books publishes distinctive books and gifts. From award-winning children's titles, bestselling cookbooks, and eclectic pop culture to acclaimed works of art and design, stationery, and journals, we craft publishing that's instantly recognizable for its spirit and creativity. Enjoy our publishing and become part of our community at www.chroniclebooks.com.